Follow Your Bliss!

Follow Your Bliss!

a practical, soul-centered guide
to job-hunting and career-life planning

by

Helen Nienhaus Barba

Universal Publishers/uPUBLISH.com
USA • 2000

Published by
Universal Publishers/uPUBLISH.com
USA • 2000

ISBN: 1-58112-746-4

www.upublish.com/books/barba.htm

For Mom and Dad

ACKNOWLEDGMENTS

This book has been working on me for many years, nurtured by the support and encouragement I have received from mentors and friends who have urged me forward to "follow my Bliss." They include (in consecutive order): Kimberly Gronewald Hall, Bob Goheen, Pat Hillquist, Dr. Mary J. Nicholas, Dr. Mary Preston Benson, Dr. Michael J. Cosky, Catherine Hayes, Bernie Wolfard, Richard Pimentel, Bill Murphy, Dan Shapiro, Meredith Harron, Dr. Paolo Knill, Dr. Shaun McNiff, John White, May LaVenture, and all those with whom I have sung and played at the St. Michael's Choir in Prior Lake, Minnesota. A smile warms my face as I think of you, one by one. How great the impact the lot of you have had upon my creative life!

I owe an equal debt of gratitude to my clients, and also to my most intimate peers in the discipline of expressive therapy: Elizabeth David, Eileen Feldman, Kit Jenkins, and Sara Tsutsumi. It has been a privilege to know and to work with your fine minds and imaginative souls in creating a laboratory to further define our individual therapeutic styles and ideas.

Of course, this acknowledgment would be incomplete without a mention of my husband, John and my four remarkable children, Genevieve, Sam, Jacqueline and David. Thanks for bearing with me.

CONTENTS

TABLE OF EXERCISES

FOREWORD
Creating with the Workplace
by
Shaun McNiff

Experience teaches that the great frontiers for the creative process are places where it is least recognized. Today the workplace is that unexplored region of creative discovery and practice. Both leaders and workers know that something has to change.

There is a great reservoir of creative potential that needs to be released, but we have yet to find the way. Well intentioned efforts to introduce the creative imagination into the workplace tend to be characterized by superficial outcomes such as short-lived trends of poets reading to corporate boards who feel the need for something outside the lines of work as usual. In an effort to inspire and retain talented employees, creativity consultants redesign work environments and make them more spacious, illuminated by natural light, and open to the natural world. All of these efforts are important steps toward a deeper experience of reality, but the technician mentality that drives the workplace today is simply incapable of contacting the undiscovered resources of the creative imagination that lie waiting in individuals, groups, and places.

As I was preparing a lecture on "creativity and workplace," my fourteen year old daughter said, "Daddy, those are two words that people don't usually connect to one another." My daughter is absolutely correct. Creativity is something we do, if we have the time, outside work. We imagine retirement as a period when we can finally focus on what we really want to do with our lives, and then discover that we miss the connections to people, situations, and problems that provide the interactive fuels of creation. The creative imagination is an intelligence that operates outside the lines, and the workplace is the ultimate arena for linear thought and action.

During the 17th, 18th, and early 19th centuries English and German thinkers defined the imagination as an intermediate realm that integrates rational, intuitive, and sensory knowing. The creative imagination draws together the resources of a person's different faculties and generates new things based on a transformative mix of often unlikely elements. Everything from experience, good and bad, contributes to the outcomes that lie outside the parameters of linear cause and effect. Imagination makes leaps into new ways of perceiving and engaging the world that can be likened to the discoveries of late 20th century physics.

The workplace of today has not been significantly influenced by the discoveries of the new physics. It is a realm shaped largely by the old linear science and industries that never adopted the pre-industrial visions of creative imagination. For two centuries the science of work has stayed strictly within the lines. Imagination is commonly defined as unreality, and imaginative people are viewed as escaping from the real world.

We all need our retreats from the world of work to regenerate and refocus our creative energies. There are many pathogens in the workplace in terms of stress, fear, and monotony. My experience constantly indicates that the things that oppress us the most carry the seeds of major transformations of consciousness. I realize that I need the community of people within the workplace and our collaborative efforts toward shared goals to keep me connected to the real stuff of life. I create together with the world and not completely apart from it. Work and daily life offer the "stuff" of creative imagination and especially the irritants and problems that push the creative process into new frontiers of engagement.

As the human resource director at my workplace said to me, "Creativity is very hard to cultivate in the workplace and very easy to destroy." She went on to describe how fear is the primary threat to creative expression at work. What happens if I take a risk and it goes against the grain of workplace values? What will I do if I lose this job?

Creative imagination requires us to place things in new relationships and to go beyond the boundaries of how things are presently done, whereas the workplace typically requires the opposite from people. How can these contradictions be addressed? Is there hope for the practice of creative imagination in the workplace? Even though it may be widely recognized that creativity is good for the workplace, that it fosters greater productivity and invention, helps people to feel better about themselves and their jobs, and thoroughly energizes environments, it may be viewed as counter-culture, threatening the command and control systems that drive contemporary business. Companies and organizations are simply not set-up to deliver the creative process. Too much creativity can actually get you into trouble within environments where you are expected to stay completely within the lines and meet standardized expectations.

There are many aspects of work that require strict adherence to rules and regulations and linear problem solving. The practice of imagination in the workplace must ultimately work together with boundaries and concrete expectations. It is not a matter of embracing one without the other. Experience indicates that restrictions can often feed creation so long as there is a receptivity to divergent possibilities and new discoveries. Leadership needs to model respect for new ideas and make it safe for people to experiment and try something different.

Paradigm inconsistencies can evaporate immediately when we discover that something new works and offers great value. Therefore the contradictions between imaginative and linear thinking are not insurmountable. I believe the ongoing separation between creativity and work results from a comprehensive inability to grasp what can be done differently. Simply stated, we know that the practice of creation can be good for the workplace, but we don't know how to do it. Superficial gimmicks will do more to undermine the practice of imagination and keep it outside organizational life.

I believe that it will be the efforts of inspired individuals that will bring about the integration of work and creative imagination. People guided by visions can change anything. As increasing numbers of people begin to share the same vision and work toward it together, it becomes a consensually validated reality. The primary force for change in the workplace will be the consciousness of workers who feel that something very important is lacking in their lives.

We typically say that the infusion of imagination into the workplace depends upon visionary leaders who establish and hold the space for others to create. The role of leadership is crucial, but I believe that sweeping changes in organization life are more apt to occur through a rising tide of worker aspirations. When these positive shifts in consciousness occur, leadership manifests a responsive intelligence that helps the innovations take root and grow.

Helen Nienhaus Barba's book is one of these inspired and important individual contributions to a larger change in consciousness. The author knows that something is missing in the world and she has taken action to doing something different. Her book is based upon Joseph Campbell's exhortation to "follow your bliss." As John Lennon said, "imagine all the people," following their instincts about how to create a better and more complete life. I also have no doubt that a more blissful experience at work will be more productive and good for the bottom line, but we still don't know how to go about doing this.

Barba offers many practical steps toward realizing a more productive and creative relationship with work. This book reads both like a challenge and a common sense course of action:

. Stretch the imagination and watch how it changes the realities that appear beyond our control.

. There is a power in the practice of imagination that has yet to be tapped.

. Everything depends upon how we think about things.

. Pay attention to the things that bother you and actually "indulge" them, Barba says. See your problems as doorways to change. They are telling you what needs attention.

. Work can be a labor of the heart, the author says, and this power can be channeled in new ways.

In addition to giving a big picture of a new relationship to work, Barba offers many practical tips on resume writing, job counseling, goal setting, prioritizing, and so forth. Ultimately it is the sustained application of the creative imagination to these ordinary things that really changes the world. The realization of a more creatively fulfilling workplace is based upon what Barba calls "intuitions of the future" and new possibilities of what we can do within organizational life.

Helen Nienhaus Barba is making her individual contribution to the rising tide of creativity in the workplace. Read this book and discover what *you* can do. Following your bliss is often difficult. Setbacks and disappointments are inevitably on the way to creating something new. The sense of bliss is the vision, the guide, and the affirmation that something different is possible. It is not just momentary pleasure. Bliss can be a beautiful idea of what can someday exist. Trust your "intuitions of the future" and be assured that the creative process can ultimately deliver you to a new place.

This book's focus on the workplace challenges us all to work together to revision and recreate the place that binds us all.

PREFACE

I'll do anything. I don't care about a career.
I just need a job.
-- Anonymous

Life is too short to be spent at a job that holds no personal value -- or, in the worst case scenario, at a job that evokes apathy, misery or contempt. And yet, many of us feel painfully insecure about our abilities to find meaning and satisfaction in work.

On the other hand, there is Joe the Conductor. In workshops I held in Massachusetts I often spoke about Joe. I never knew his real name, but I knew his presence well. He rode the commuter rail between Boston and Fitchburg, Massachusetts, and he lived and breathed his job so naturally, and with such pride, that it was nearly impossible to imagine him in any other role. I could tell by the proud way he sauntered through the aisles and bellowed out his stops that he loved his job. The most amazing thing was that the moment I began to describe Joe during my workshops, at least one or two people in the room who had ridden the rail knew exactly whom I meant.

Joe the Conductor was one of those fortunate individuals who had found a way to "follow his Bliss," to borrow a phrase from the late Joseph Campbell. I have grown fond of the term "Bliss." Webster defines Bliss as "perfect happiness" and "heavenly joy," which implies a spiritual connection. The word is originally derived from the Greek word *bhlei*, meaning "to shine." For me, Bliss arrives in grace-filled moments when I am me most completely: when I lose track of time in the midst of a creative endeavor, when a tragedy calls forth strengths I didn't know I had, when a stunning sunset prompts me to pause and consider my place in the universe. Bliss even accompanies rare moments when I let down my guard and face my inadequacies.

In the pages to follow I hope to make the path to Bliss accessible to *you*, and to advance the notions that:

(1) like everyone, you *deserve* more than a "just a job"; you deserve Bliss.

(2) you *have the potential to achieve* Bliss.

(3) you have an *obligation* to make use of the gifts and talents which uniquely equip you for work that nurtures the soul, and incidentally leads to Bliss.

It's easy to acknowledge that everyone deserves joy and satisfaction in his or her work. Still, many behave as if they *don't* deserve it. The phenomenon seems to have sprouted in part from puritanical roots which framed work as drudgery to be performed with perseverance and humility, but not necessarily with enjoyment, nor (heaven forbid) with passion.

The attitude is reflected in the way we use language to describe work. We make clear distinctions between "work" and "play." And those who dare to admit, "I *love* this job -- I can't believe they pay me to do this!" can meet with disapproval, envy, or derision. Some even feel inclined to *apologize* for enjoying their work.

When people view joy and passion in work as a luxury – or, worse yet, as mutually exclusive terms -- it is not surprising that they approach the job search with low expectations.   Paradoxically, this positioning actually works against the job seeker. Rather than facing greater numbers of opportunities -- which some assume an I'll-take-anything approach will yield -- we more often find ourselves immobilized, without direction, and *unable to inspire the involvement and help of others.* Success, as it turns out, characteristically *eludes* those who lack the focus and direction which a follow-your-Bliss posture can provide.

Follow Your Bliss! supports the search for purposeful, meaningful, satisfying work with a series of exercises and words of inspiration. It is best studied and worked on within a small group, or at least with a partner. I have found that dialog between people inspires imagination and makes the work richer. The ideal arrangement, in my view, is for individuals and groups to work in partnership with an expressive therapist -- a masters level clinician/psychotherapist with special training in the use and interpretation of artistic as well as verbal expressions.*

Most of all, the quest requires generous measures of imagination and courage. Each of these qualities deserves further mention here.

The Power of Imagination

Let me begin by sharing a basic, governing principle:

The way we imagine ourselves has far more power in our lives than the way we literally are.

---

*To learn more about expressive therapy, contact the International Expressive Arts Therapy Association (IEATA) at P.O. Box 641246, San Francisco, California 94164-1246.

It is the way we imagine ourselves -- not any fantasy we have about an "objective" or literal reality -- that plays the dominant role in dictating how we behave. The eating disorder *anorexia nervosa* provides a striking and sobering example. Our vision of a beautiful, young woman literally wasting away by deliberately starving herself simply does not match the girl's own vision of a grossly overweight person. For her, refusing to eat is not so simple as a cry for attention; it actually arises from an *altered way of imagining reality.* The girl behaves in full accordance with her perceived reality.

Another example more relevant to the career search can be found in a story from writer and philosopher Sam Keen. In an interview with Bill Moyers (*Sam Keen: Your Mythic Journey,* 1991), Dr. Keen told of his high achiever brother who had developed a reputation in the family for superior mechanical ability. Young Sam saw himself in comparison as someone who could never quite measure up. As an adult, he took an achievement test in the hopes of getting guidance in choosing a job. When the counselor presented him with the results, he was not surprised to hear that his scores fell "in the fifth percentile." "That sounds about right," Sam conceded. "Ninety-five percent of the people tested scored better than I did." "No, no," replied the counselor. "You're in the *top* five percent. Ninety-five percent scored *below* you." Sam answered, "No -- that's my brother." From an early age, he had *imagined* that he lacked mechanical ability, and this imagination strongly influenced his behavior.

The power of imagination, though it can present obstacles, is a great gift. The implication is that if you give yourself permission to imagine yourself doing what you love most, doing it well and enjoying success, you come that much closer to actually being there. This is no trick. It is a legitimate tool for accessing a realm far more powerful and just as real as our literal reality. There are those who insist that they have killed cancers by imagining them gone -- not as a fleeting imagining, but repeatedly, with faith and with great detail (Siegel, 1986). How much more difficult can it be to land a job *for which you are uniquely suited?*

On the other hand, if you imagine that you have no hope of ever finding happiness in a job, guess what? This becomes your reality. There *is* no hope, not because of any literal reality, but because of how you imagine your reality. If you imagine hopelessness, how can you put more than a half-hearted effort into a job search? By the same token, what employer will want to hire someone with a hopeless attitude?

The phenomenon of the power of imagination holds true not only for individuals, but also for the collective awareness of our culture. As a case in point, *consumer confidence* has a huge impact on our economy, and it is as simple as this: When we have confidence, we spend. When we spend, we feed the economy. And when we feed the economy, it grows. A "weak" economy can only be *aided* when consumer confidence is high and leads to increased spending. On the other hand, no amount of wealth stashed away will help an economy when its keeper lacks confidence in his employability and/or in the capacity of the economy to meet his need for meaningful employment.

Several years ago, we were all bathed in a nationwide sense of hopelessness and doom. The economy was "bad." This is was the social reality we imagined for ourselves. In a period of time when the economy is characterized as "bad," the psychological impact can be broad and exaggerated. We often imagine things to be worse than they are. The psychological impact is loss of hope, and it dictates our behavior and hurts us more than any literal reality can.

What's more, hopelessness can prevent us from hearing the *good* news. And there *has* been good news, even during our bleakest periods. In the midst of our "bad economy," between 1970 and 1980, for example, the number of available jobs in the United States actually rose by over twenty million, and in 1986 we added another ten million (Wegmann et. al., 1989, p. 7). Unemployment ran high for a time only because of an increase in people *seeking* work, most notably a flood of baby boomers, immigrants, and women. This sudden, uneven growth put the *mix* of jobs in flux. As the economy grew stronger, the unemployment rate continued to decline.

Sadly, many people have failed to adjust their expectations even with improving economic conditions. This is understandable in part because of the difficulty in comprehending and adapting to monumental changes in the nature of work and the workforce. But before I address these changes -- a word about courage.

Courage

As the reader can well imagine by now, a fertile and active imagination cannot propel a person on the path to soul-nurturing work without a generous measure of courage. There are certain to be obstacles on this path, moments of doubt, and fear.

For the most part, fear cannot be avoided. Courage has been defined as the ability to *Feel the Fear and Do It Anyway* (Jeffers, 1987). Courage means stretching past the safe boundaries of a daily routine and rising to meet the challenges that call you. This can be mighty scary. But as the saying goes, if you're never scared, then you can never know true courage.

Many need help to muster the courage and confidence required to manage and thrive within the new economy and to follow Bliss. Sometimes the first step may be to muster the courage to ask for help -- from a career counselor, therapist, professional resumé writer, or even from a friend. But taking this first step is only the beginning, for fear has the tendency to return to haunt us. I'll come back to this point in greater depth in Step Five, found in the latter part of the book.

For now, in order to thrive in a changing economy and world, we must "reimagine the game" and our role in it.

STEP ONE:
RE-IMAGINING THE GAME

*Everything we know and feel
and every statement we make
[is] fantasy-based; that is,
[everything] derives from psychic images.*
-- James Hillman

Today our economy is stronger, inflation is low, and productivity is up. As the unemployment rate has declined, industries which were hungry for workers all along have become starved to fill positions in which extensive growth has taken place. Meanwhile, many job seekers stand at the periphery, facing the wrong way, feeling ill equipped to traverse the gulf between themselves and a much desired sense of security imagined as long-term employment. Surely, they imagine, some company will take care of them; if only they knew where to go to get the "new skills" they require.

Unfortunately, the answer is not straightforward. In most cases, when the iron mill closed, another iron mill did not open up on the other side of town. Neither did a different kind of mill open, requiring a simple upgrade of skills to operate new machines. Perhaps nothing opened up at all! The fact is, not only have the *rules* of the game changed, the entire game has changed. What worked twenty, ten, or even five years ago does not work anymore.

What is important here is not whether you characterize changes in the economy as "good" or "bad," but that you understand the new shape of an economy which has experienced a monumental transformation. It is important that you explore how to maneuver within it and further influence its development. People with talents exist, and in the wisdom in the universe, *needs* for individual talents also exist. The bringing together of the two is a most natural phenomenon.

But the jobs in many cases have yet to be defined. In this day and age, you must take greater responsibility to define your own position. It may seem a foreboding task, but it is also an exciting opportunity. For even on a global scale, the power of individuals to imagine possibilities can have an enormous impact. One day not so long ago, one person had an idea about an unheard of thing called "fast food," and now the world's landscape is covered with golden arches!**

**I suspect that many had the same idea of creating a speedy, affordable alternative to restaurants and diners, for this is the way of global change. But only one person had the courage and wherewithal to act on the idea in a way that has changed all our lives. I will discuss this phenomenon in greater depth in Step Four.

The Way We Imagine Employers

Once upon a time, a dominant myth of the workplace held that middle-class Americans could depend upon their employers to take care of them. It was not at all unusual for an individual to offer up the services of his labor to a company, which in return would offer long-term security, defined as a job to go to every day, a stable income, a pension to which one could look forward. The rapid pace of our current economy, including the tenuousness with which companies thrive from day to day, has necessitated a change in this myth.

Our values have changed as well. When mass production was the preferred method of manufacturing goods (as opposed to individualized, customized and personalized service) employers placed a high value on loyalty and conformity among workers. Now we are in a new age. Growth companies today recognize that it is much more profitable for them to place a higher value on qualities in their workers such as originality, imagination, and an entrepreneurial spirit.

It is natural to react to this change as a frightening and unwanted thing. Moreover, it seems to be a temptation for many to cast blame upon the Employer (with a capital "e") for the state of affairs, for it is the Employer who has assumed the more

Oh, Great Employer, I am not worthy!

powerful role in the past. In an archetypal sense, this phenomenon of being forced out of a corporate "nest" or comfort zone can be experienced as facing abandonment by the Father.

In shifting from a myth which values reliance on an external caretaker to one which necessitates *self* reliance, you must change the way you imagine employers and the way you imagine yourself and your roles. Ultimately the way you choose careers and move within the job market is determined by your expectations. Many of us sense this instinctively. We know that we can no longer depend upon the Employer for a sense of security. You may also deduce that any hope of enjoying security no longer exists. Not so! With the changing myth, you must simply seek and find security elsewhere; namely, within yourself.

A few years ago I created a cartoon to illustrate to some job developers I was training how many of us imagine our employers (see figure below). Notice how much power the illustration gives the employer. Can you imagine what would happen if we reversed the image? How would that look and feel?

In fact, the relationship works best when a sense of equality is conveyed. But many of us need to let the pendulum swing far to the other side, and puff ourselves up a bit, before we are able to feel comfortable with a partnership.

Imagine the implications of this different world view. Suddenly, you are not coming to an employer expecting that she will be doing you a *favor* by hiring you. Instead, you are genuinely aware of how lucky she'll be to have you. And that is not just a mind game; it is a true interpretation of the facts. People who work for companies are hired to do so in this day and age because of their distinct abilities to contribute. They become need-meeters and profit-earners. The most successful are those who are proactive and entrepreneurial in their approach.

Denise Bissonnette describes an entrepreneurial approach in her book, *Beyond Traditional Job Development*, which is chock full of wisdom and ideas for job developers negotiating in today's job market. She explains a method she calls "applicant focused job creation," which consists of four essential steps (Bissonnette, 1994, pp. 44-57):

(1) Assess the needs a person can meet given their skills, abilities and total life experience.

(2) Identify organizations which have those needs.

(3) Identify how the employer will profit from hiring the person.

(4) Make a verbal or written employment proposal.

The same method can be applied to an independent job search. An important thing here is to not get hung up on the prospect of creating a formal, written proposal each time you apply for a job. Some circumstances may require a written proposal, or it may be useful to write something up for the purpose of clarifying your thoughts. However, your mind set is what matters most: taking primary responsibility for figuring out what you have to offer and engaging your imagination to come up with ideas which you can then communicate convincingly and with confidence.

The Way We Imagine Ourselves

When we imagine employers as our caretakers, we tend to attach our identities -- or at least our career identities -- to them. When we shift to a mode of self reliance, our identity becomes more personal.

Here is a simple exercise to try. Imagine that you are currently working as a salesperson for a multimillion dollar corporation called Springfield Important Computers (SIC). SIC has a reputation for taking extremely good care of its people. It typically takes people with limited education and skills, trains them in their own particular language and methods, and promotes them to high-paying, salaried positions.

Suppose now that you find yourself at a party -- a dance, cocktail party, wedding. As you are introduced to other party goers, think about how you might respond to the question, "What do you do?" Look at the continuum of statements below. Now ask yourself,

---

EXAMPLE 1

1. "I'm a 'SIC-y.'"
2. "I work for Springfield Important Computers."
3. "I sell software for SIC."
4. "I'm a salesperson in a large corporation."
5. "I'm a computer buff with a knack for selling user-friendly software to computer-unfriendly people."
6. "I'm a full-time dad, a part-time computer buff, and I make the best chili in Springfield."

- Which *type* of statement have you used most in your experience?
- Which one *fits* you best?
- Which one would you *like* to use more?

I purposely chose a corporation with a reputation for being a powerful company that "takes good care of its people." Employers of this sort are particularly hard to separate from. For people who work for such powerful companies, there is a nearly irresistible urge to name the company by way of introduction. People thrive within these cultures, for a time. But many devoted employees of such large companies have experienced huge layoffs since the 1980s. The casualties have a tougher time than most in readjusting and getting back into the workforce. The unique culture and language of former employers can become so ingrained that people may struggle to get a handle on and articulate what they have to offer elsewhere. Their resumés stand out from others'; they read like SIC resumés. The emotional impact is perhaps the most devastating legacy of all. Being abandoned by the powerful Father and facing the never-suspected prospect of having to suddenly find another way to be "taken care of" can be a terrifying experience, and it can require an extended period of healing.

Returning to our imaginary scenario, suppose you are that corporate salesperson again and you have just been laid off. Now what do you say at the party? It may take some time before you are able to shed the SIC identity -- to move from "I used to be a SICy" to "I'm a dad, a computer buff, and a great chili maker." It is a process of realizing "I am not my job; I am *more* than my job." **It is easier to move into another job from the *latter***

attitude.

For most, there are many avenues through which potentials can be fulfilled and gifts can be used. In the final analysis, the success you experience today depends less on who helps you than upon who you are, and on how this measures up against how you have defined "success" for yourself.

Imagining Success

Let's turn briefly to a discussion of what it means to be successful. It may be helpful to begin with an exercise. All it requires is a plain sheet of paper and some thought.

EXERCISE 1: **HOW I IMAGINE SUCCESS**

1. Take a sheet of paper oriented horizontally. Along the lefthand margin, make a list of 5-7 things *you* feel are essential to success.
2. Across the top of the page, write the numbers 1-6. This will be a rating scale, with 6 being high.
3. Now rate yourself on each of the items, reflecting upon *where you are today*.
4. Connect the dots.

Look at the example on the following page. Note how this individual (we'll call her Jane) has defined success. Based on her definition, she is partially successful, since she has evaluated herself as being bright, with a lot of good friends and excellent typing skills. She further assesses herself as being not very persistent, even less assertive, having few connections, and being virtually broke. Put yourself in Jane's shoes. What would you do?

To most people, the answer seems obvious. Traditional wisdom would probably have Jane grabbing the first job she sees in order to get some immediate income, taking a class in assertiveness training, and cold-calling around to make some of those "networking" connections she now feels are so important.

EXAMPLE 2	1	2	3	4	5	6
1. Money	•					
2. Connections		•				
3. Assertiveness		•				
4. Good friends						•
5. Typing skills						•
6. Intelligence					•	
7. Persistence				•		

Suppose Jane tries all these things. What do you expect will happen? In my experience, it often follows a course something like this: Jane immediately starts working at a convenience store down the street. (It's the first job she sees.) She works alone most of the time, feels insecure about her work, since it's new to her, but keeps telling herself it's only temporary. In the evenings, she takes an assertiveness training class in which the teacher encourages her to "think positively and speak up for herself." She also teaches her to stand up straight and use her voice in a way that seems more confident and direct. The class is extremely difficult for Jane; she feels like a fish out of water and is in awe of her instructor. She has never been very persistent, and she thinks about quitting, but she fears that this is her only hope. As for the cold-calls, she has good intentions to make them, but she never seems to get around to it and is secretly plagued by guilt over this "failure."

Meanwhile, Jane *neglects her strengths* -- her typing skills and small circle of friends. A few weeks later, she rates herself on the same scale and finds that except for a small increase in her income, everything else on the scale has actually gotten worse! What happened?

Well, let's suppose Jane had taken the *opposite* approach. Suppose she invested *all* of her attention and energies into those things for which gave herself high ratings. Let's suppose, for example, that she dusted off her word processor, got hold of some software she had never used but always wanted to learn, and started typing two to three hours a day. Let's also suppose she made a point of calling at least one *friend* each day and planning two outings a week.

The fact is, chances are good that the *entire scale* would improve. Jane would find that in addition to increasing her typing speed to eighty-five words per minute with zero errors, and in addition to learning a new word processing program, she would discover an increased assertiveness in herself *that emerged as a natural byproduct of engaging in an activity she already enjoyed and in which she already felt confident.* And she would find that by engaging her closest friends in discussions about her hopes and dreams, she would have sparked *their* imaginations, gotten them involved in her job search, and thereby expanded her personal network, or "connections," to use her term. It's also likely that a more fitting job would follow.

My purpose in this exercise is to help support people's confidence in following Bliss and fueling existing strengths. It's a wholeness-based approach, as opposed to a deficit-based approach (which focuses on fixing what's wrong) or even an abundance-based approach (Bissonnette). Following it requires some re-learning, since popular culture seems intent upon guiding people towards "self improvement," towards finding what is wrong and fixing or eliminating it. **Let us begin with the radical assumption that *nothing is wrong*.** Rather, things are as they are, and our challenge is to make the most of what we have.

Re-framing Strengths and Weaknesses

Just out of undergraduate school I took a job that I loved. The only drawback to the position was finding myself in a somewhat tense relationship with the director of the agency in which my program was housed. We were able to work together pretty well despite our different styles. Then, as a courtesy, my outside supervisor invited the agency director's input in my performance review.

I had done outstanding work since hired, and the

performance review reflected that. However, at the very end of the review form, under "areas in need of improvement," I found myself taken aback when I read the agency director's comment that I was inclined to be "aloof" around staff.

I was young and ambitious and eager to do well, and the comment took the wind out of my sails. It seemed to me that this person had gone out of her way to find something to complain about, but I set aside my astonishment, anger, and pride and chose to examine what grain of truth might lie in those words.

After some reflection, I was able to understand how the director might have arrived at the remark. I knew that I was able to bring a very attentive presence to the *clients* with whom I worked; however, I was not the type of person who was inclined to socialize at the water fountain. Most of the time, I dove into my work with a deliberateness and concentration that left little time for lunch and bathroom breaks, never mind small-talk. It was easy for me to imagine myself busily writing at a computer terminal and not even noticing a passerby offering a morning greeting. Could this be interpreted as aloofness? Probably. How far was I willing to go to change myself? Not very far. I was unwilling to give up a part of myself that had served me so well in my life. I could certainly make an effort to make my personal style known to people so that they would not feel that I was purposely snubbing them. I could even make an effort to take a break once in a while to check on how other people were doing. But I refused on principle to become someone I was not. Giving up this quality would have meant giving up a gift I had for completing huge volumes of work with great efficiency, and I still had a lot of work I wanted to do.

What I learned from this experience was that **we all have dominant qualities which can be malleable to a certain extent but which also help to define us as individuals.** These dominant qualities can be our greatest strengths *as well as* our greatest weaknesses. They are qualities which have many aspects. It will behoove you to take stock of them and acquaint yourself with them, so that you can better assess what *you* have to offer the world -- and better communicate it. Ultimately, this awareness helps in finding your most fitting niche. You are certainly better off in terms of your personal happiness and also in terms of the betterment of the world when you fully embrace the unique individual that you are.

On the following page is an exercise to help you get started in gaining access to knowledge of your dominant qualities through the "weakness" aspect.

Sadly, many people seem to be far more aware of -- and in some cases obsessed with -- their perceived weaknesses than their strengths. This is often the easiest or quickest point of access to understanding dominant qualities -- most notably for people with low self esteem.

Let's walk through an example. Suppose Carlos feels uncomfortable in large groups of people he does not know well. He shares an apartment with a gregarious gentleman, George, who frequently boasts of all the great contacts he makes at parties and networking events. George serves as a relentless reminder to Carlos of his own tendency to shy away from large groups, and Carlos perceives this trait as a weakness.

After identifying his "weakness," Carlos begins by meticulously painting an image of a room full of "upwardly mobile" men and women bearing cell phones

---

EXERCISE #2: **EXPLORING DOMINANT QUALITIES**

1. Think about a personal trait that you have
    defined as a "weakness."
2. Externalize the thing and give it substance. That
    is, draw it, shape it in a lump of clay, write a
    poem that captures its different aspects. Take
    some time to reflect upon your creation.
3. Describe the thing to someone else, and/or write
    down your description (In other words, define it
    outside of your identified present.) Ask yourself
    the following questions about it:
    • What is it?
    •   How did it originate? (That is, are you sure
        that it's really yours, or did it come from
        someone else's ideas about you?)
    •   How does it *serve* you?
    •   What challenges, opportunities or dangers
        does it present?
    •   How do you, or can you, compensate for its
        other side? Its shadow?
    •   If it could speak, what might it say?
    •   What does it have to teach?
    •   What does it have that you need?

---

and buzzing with conversation. He places himself in a
corner with his back to the wall and a look of terror on
his face. (Already this rich material lends opportunities to
learn a great deal about Carlos -- his careful manner, his
ability to manipulate art materials skillfully, the fact that
he doesn't particularly care for the type of cell-phone-

toting people portrayed in his image, who on further reflection seem shallow and self-serving to him.)

When asked to be more specific about his "shyness" and what *it* looks like, Carlos elaborates: "Shyness hovers in the room. It is a cloud, a barrier between me and the rest." A dialog ensues: How does the barrier serve you? "It protects me from being taken in by people I cannot trust." Does the barrier follow you everywhere? "No, only in places where I feel vulnerable." Describe the cloud in more detail. "Soft -- like cotton, but I can put my hand through it. I could even walk right through it if I wished." It sounds pleasant, and as though you have some control over it. "Yes. It's actually quite warm and comforting." If it could speak to you, what do you think the cloud would say? "Hello there, Carlos!" So the barrier is more friend than foe? What if it did not exist? "Hmm — I really think I need it there."

This is an abbreviated version of a dialog that could lend more and more insights when pursued further. But already it is clear that Carlos' "shyness" serves him by offering a protective boundary that he can, in fact, penetrate when he wishes to connect with others. We all need boundaries, and not all of us manage them as well as Carlos. Can you think of any occupations where this attribute might be an asset? How about a person who must deal with sensitive or confidential material?

Take heed from this example. It is so important to make the most of who we are, for the universe requires us all. Imagine how dull and uninspired life would be if we were able to change our basic attributes with the push of a button, eliminating the ones we find too challenging. Imagine the lessons we'd never learn, the joys we'd never know.

What Personality Is Not

Be careful here not to confuse *traits* with *feelings*. Personality traits are predispositions that help to define individuals. As a rule, they are unchangeable. They might include introversion, charisma, or a natural affinity for working with animals. On the other hand, things like laziness, lack of motivation and lack of enthusiasm are not personality traits at all, but *feelings*, very much dependent on circumstances.

Time and again people we know counsel us about what employers want: enthusiasm, commitment, initiative, motivation, stick-to-it-iveness, to name a few. Too often, we think of these qualities as personality traits. In other words, we either have them, or we don't. In fact, all these traits lie within every human being's repertoire. We may manifest them in different ways, but regardless of our style in expressing enthusiasm, for example, people will recognize it when they witness it. Enthusiasm is a natural human ability. **It is not a function of personality; it is a function of *how we feel*.**

This is very good news, indeed! For it means that these highly valued attitudes are within everyone's reach. Think about a time in your life when you were enthusiastic about something. If you have never felt enthusiasm, I feel badly for you, but hear this: It is not because of *who you are*. It is because of *how you feel*. Perhaps no one has ever given you reason or hope for whatever it is that sparks your enthusiasm. I am giving you permission now. I insist upon it. Remember, it is not only your *right* to know Bliss and to pursue it, but it is also your *responsibility*. You are robbing the rest of the world as well as yourself if you ignore it.

Remembering times in our lives when we felt tuned in to our truest sense of ourselves is a critical step in the career search, and many of the career-life planning exercises in this book are based upon this premise. I will share a few of these in Step Three.

STEP TWO:
COMING TO TERMS WITH THE MISERY

*If I stay in this job, I'm afraid I'll end up hurting
someone.
I'm so filled with rage -- and these days
it doesn't take much to set me off.*

Harry was a story on the evening news waiting to happen when he came to the first meeting of the More-than-a-Job Club seminar. I was accustomed to beginning these seminars by giving people the opportunity to indulge in an initial "gripe session." I wasn't sure that the holding environment I had created in the seminar structure was adequate for containing the rage Harry brought with him, and I considered making a referral to some outside counseling. But in this case, the group turned out to be a small one, able to quickly establish a trusting environment by demonstrating an eagerness to accompany this troubled soul on his quest.

Harry's story was one of being denied a promotion which had been given instead to a younger gentleman with an inside connection to the company, a man whom Harry felt was less competent. Harry had come to the seminar with the intent of getting out of the situation as soon as he could, before he did something he might regret.

In the first session, each member of the group exorcized feelings of dissatisfaction and anger, not only with words, but in creative writing and art work as well. The following week, we began the process of in-depth self-inventorying. At about that time, Harry reported a startling change at his workplace. He no longer dreaded showing up for work, no longer feared losing control, was able to leave his work "at the office," and actually found small ways to enjoy some of his work while there. His only explanation for the change was the cathartic and therapeutic impact of putting his anger out on the table.

When you feel unrest or "dissonance," this is a direct cue for you to pause and reassess. There is no way around this pause, no way to rush the process. Later on, you may choose to betray what you have discovered or uncovered, but you will never be able to ignore it. Every time we try to avoid the things that haunt us, they simply return with greater insistence.

As an expressive therapist, I appreciate the value of externalizing words and images and containing them in artistic material in order to enable people to relate to the images in new ways, and to deepen their understanding of the myths and dynamics described in them (Barba, *A Psychology of Recurring Imagery*, 1988; Knill, Barba, & Fuchs, *Minstrels of Soul*, 1993). I watched as Harry stood back and regarded the material he had put out, and we all listened with interest as he talked about what he wrote and sketched. We did not "analyze" the words and images, we simply witnessed their evolution. For they were not stuck anymore like a broken record; they were dynamic entities which became richer with each new comment and observation.

Garrett McAuliffe ("Career as an Imaginative Quest," 1993, p. 36) calls this first, cathartic stage of career exploration "acknowledging dissonant voices." I have found this to be a critical stage which serves several important purposes:

(1) It permits a cleansing catharsis of feelings of anger,

disappointment, guilt, frustration, confusion and/or whatever else might be demanding attention.

(2) It allows for the initial development of rapport between people; opportunities to listen and support each other.

(3) It opens the door to *change;* that is, when you confront how awful things are, it becomes more difficult to ignore them and do nothing.

(4) It allows for the development of a more complete perspective on one's situation, or the ability to see the "big picture"; e.g., I am not my anger. I am more than my anger.

(5) It offers some initial insights into what has not worked in the past and, therefore, what might work better in the future.

(6) It facilitates the letting go of and moving on from places of stasis.

This is the time to *indulge the negative.* It is not the time to rush forward into "getting over it" or "making nice." The unpleasant material requires a fair hearing and full acknowledgment before an individual can move on to problem-solve and set new goals. There is much to be learned in the telling of and dialoging with "tales of woe."

Again, I encourage the use of art at this stage in the process. I have found that presenting material in a collage or sculpture can be liberating and for some much easier than trying to find words to convey painful stories and the feelings they arouse. When images emerge, they always bring new, sometimes surprising information and, especially in dialog, a richer and fuller understanding of the issue being addressed. These same images can become familiar touchstones which return at various stages of the career search to inform our perspective on struggles, stumbling blocks and successes.

STEP THREE:
ART AND THE WAY TO SELF AWARENESS

You need to remember it's your life.
-- Barbara Sher

There is a fundamental flaw in the way that career assessment has traditionally been conducted. Typically, an individual is interviewed and/or given a test consisting of multiple choice questions. Personal interviews are less formal and structured. But in both cases, inquiries are made of the *intellect*.

When the intellect is engaged, the responses we get can be misleading. Think about a personal experience you may have had with career assessment and guidance. Call to mind those popular checklists of "values," for example. Imagine how you might proceed through the list of values named and check off or prioritize those that you find most important and least important; for example, "love" gets a number one, "money" gets a number two, and "security" gets a number three. Then someone comes up with a new list with different options, and you start to reconsider your responses. You might be inclined to think, "Creativity -- I hadn't thought of that. That's important too. Let me re-do my list."

Another problem with this approach is the tendency for the intellect to zero in on things we have been told or taught. If someone is taught that money is important and that being an accountant leads to money, and if he never questions it, not only will he name it as an important value, but he might actually proceed with getting a degree and job in accounting, even while hating it every step of the way.

Questions of life and career are not questions of the intellect.   They are questions of the heart. Therefore, the only insights into Bliss, purpose, mission, talents, interests, and values that I trust are those which are accessed not through the intellect, but through the heart, the feeling center.

Nice idea perhaps, but how is it done?

The approach I use is to **begin any inquiry not with what someone *thinks* but with how that person *feels*.** The best way to illustrate is through some more exercises, like the writing and drawing exercises included in this chapter.

Incidentally, at this stage in the process, when one engages in self exploration, the purpose is to gather in as much information as possible and not rush to define, "nail down" and consequently limit one's options. Later on, when endeavoring to "give substance to images which emerge" (the subject of Step Four), it will become more important to focus and to narrow options. This initial exploratory stage is a time for "stirring the soup." It is a time for being open and receptive to memories, images, and ideas, and to trust that if they have arrived at your doorstep, then they have purpose and meaning, even though you may not fully understand the ramifications or purpose at the time. Make room!

Who Am I, and What Does It Matter?

Individuals are many things, and there are many ways to frame who you are. I will focus here on three pertinent dimensions: values, interests and talents.

Values

We *value* what is important to us. Values may be culturally shaped to a certain extent, but they are also highly personal, and we hold on to our values with great intensity and emotion. **Values define our limits.** They form the lines past which we will not cross. This provides a useful image to help you get in touch with your values. In short, **you can get in touch with your values by examining those line-crossing moments which arouse the most intense feelings.**

EXERCISE 3: **VALUES**

Values have to do with limits. They are the lines we draw around ourselves, beyond which we will not cross without risking feelings of guilt, psychic pain, or injury. This exercise is designed to help uncover those values of greatest personal importance.

1. Put yourself in a state in which you can imagine experiencing a "line-crossing" feeling -- a feeling of righteousness or intense disapproval.

2. Now, try to recall or imagine a memory, scene, or experience that fits the feeling. Imagine as many as 4-5 of these scenes if you can.

3. Take some time to fully explore each of these scenes. Write about them in detail, drawing visual images, too, as they emerge. (You will no doubt require more space and material that is provided here.)

"Line Crossing" Scene #1

"Line Crossing" Scene #2

"Line Crossing" Scene #3

"Line Crossing" Scene #4

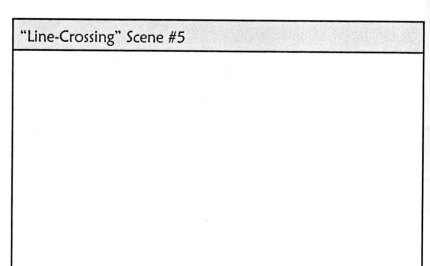

"Line-Crossing" Scene #5

4.   Now, name each of your scenes and list them in the first column in the table below.

5.   Examine each scene you have listed, and one at a time go through and explore the source of your distress. That is, what is it about this scene, specifically, which causes you to feel such intense disapproval? Write this in the appropriate box in the second column.

6.   Finally, the exploration should lead to some sense of the value implied for each story or scene. Write each value in the last column.

"Line'Crossing" Scene/Image	Source of Distress	Value Implied
#1		
#2		
#3		
#4		
#5		

This values exercise is designed to help increase your awareness of your values. I will detail the instructions and offer examples here.

The feelings connected with "line-crossing moments" tend to be judging feelings. For example, a feeling of being horrified by something, or a strong feeling of righteousness about the way things "should" be, which could be described by this language:

- "I'd never do that!"
- "It's just not me!"
- "I intensely disapprove of that."
- "That's an 'abomination' or 'a sin' or 'a crime.'"

Once you imagine yourself in a state of being in touch with feelings of righteousness or intense disapproval, stories and scenes may flash to mind. You might imagine, for example:

- a scene in which a mother is beating her child in a grocery store.
- a childhood memory of being treated with disrespect by a teacher.
- a newspaper article about a murder or other atrocity.
- an image of someone abusing a substance like alcohol.

Most of us can read a list like this and feel some level of disapproval on every item. But those values which are most important in *defining who we are* will invariably be connected with the most intense emotional responses. We can increase our understanding of our values, then, by remembering or imagining ourselves having intense emotional responses like the ones described, and by writing in detail about each story evoked. Using art materials to create some images can add detail and richness to the exploration. The more specific and thorough you can be, the more material you have to explore and learn from.

After fully exploring these stories and scenes, you are then ready to engage the intellect by examining each item and exploring the meaning in it. A useful next question (answered in the second column of the Values exercise) is, "What is the *source* of my strong feelings about this?" The answer leads to a clearer sense of the specific value implied.

Let's examine the image of the person abusing alcohol. This is an image which many find unpalatable, but often for very different reasons. One person's strong response may be rooted in a fear of losing control; implying that "control" is something *that* person values. Another may see the image as one of polluting the body with an unwanted, unhealthy substance. For this person, the predominant value implied may be "robust physical health." Still another may be plagued by memories of a parent with alcoholism and experience the image as a frightening or violent one, or one which symbolizes a shirking of family responsibilities.

As each value becomes clear, it can be noted in the worksheet's final column. In the end, a concise list of values begins to emerge. This serves as a useful guide in a search for a meaningful vocation, job, or career. It can increase your ability to recognize shared values and also shape the kinds of questions you might choose to ask in interviews. At the very least, the increased awareness can enable an informed decision about how far you might be willing to compromise your values in a work situation.

It may be useful to include a fictitious example of a completed values chart here.

"Line-Crossing" Scene/Image	Source of Distress	Value Implied
#1 Image of woman hitting her child in a grocery store.	It happened to me. I recall the pain. Children deserve care and respect.	Care and respect for children
#2 Image of a drunk passed out on a couch.	I couldn't stand destroying my own body like that.	Robust Physical Health
#3 Memory of someone going to church in dirty cut-off jeans.	I wouldn't wear clothes like that in my own home! It's disgraceful.	Neatness/cleanliness Respect for church
#4 Sloppily-done resumé	It makes me crazy --so little care put into such an important document. There's no excuse for it!	Neatness Making a good first im-pression

Remember, values are highly individualized, and these examples may not apply to you at all. Moreover, values are by definition judgmental, and the graphic descriptions and accusatory tone used are merely tools for facilitating a process of uncovering values. The statements are not intended to offend.

After reading the chart, go back and just read through the values in the final column. Here is a person who values care and respect for children, robust physical health, neatness, cleanliness, church and making a good first impression. Does it give you an impression of what this person might be like? Does it conjure a visual image?

Interests and Talents

By this stage in the process, after thoroughly examining "dissonant voices" and "line-crossing moments," you may now be ready to indulge in exploring what I call "moments of Bliss." Just as line-crossing moments can teach us about our limits and values, moments of Bliss help us to realize what our soul yearns for, and in turn they help us to define what work best suits us.

In the introductory chapter I began to address what I mean by Bliss. To elaborate here, in a moment of Bliss, I am filled with a sense of certainty that I am doing just what I was intended to do. Often, it is a joyous or ecstatic experience -- but not *necessarily* so. A moment of intense sorrow, perhaps at the death of a loved one, can call forth deep feelings of fulfilling a purpose.

Sadly, many of us become weighed down with routines and habitual responsibilities in adulthood and go for long periods of time without the pleasure of knowing

Bliss. Sometimes we have to dig deep to retrieve memories of blissful moments. Often they emerge in childhood.

For me, moments of Bliss have come on the heals of creative impulses. These moments, for me, are meditative moments characterized by the sense that time stands still. Athletes refer to the experience as being "in the zone." I feel unstoppable in this "zone." When writing this book, for example, I typed at my computer obsessively and energetically late into the night, even though I am by nature a morning person and ordinarily run out of steam early in the evening (especially after chasing four toddlers around all day!). The settling-in after the flurry is an important part of the experience for me as well. I take time to re-read and polish a piece of writing, stare at a piece of artwork, or listen at length to a finished composition.

I urge people to explore whatever areas in their lives are most filled with passion, no matter how irrelevant they may *seem* at the time. It has been my observation that many people retrieve their memories of Bliss most readily not so much from work roles as from their personal lives. One may connect the memories of a wedding day with feelings of Bliss, for example. This kind of material can be intensely forthcoming in teaching us about ourselves as individuals -- about our passions, our values, our talents. The ability to form commitments and care for others, the need for acceptance and mutual respect, the valuing of loyalty or family or ritual, and/or a special talent for public speaking, planning or entertaining might all be implied in the Bliss that a wedding day might arouse.

The interests and talents exercise mirrors the values

exercise in that we begin with feelings and *later* engage the intellect. The process is one of (1) imagining the feeling state of Bliss, then (2) recalling or imagining scenes, stories or experiences that have accompanied such a feeling, and finally (3) exploring each scene in detail. In the detailed exploration, one engages the intellect to examine the who, what, and wheres of the images.

The exercise I use appears on the following pages. Once again, I will include a fictitious example immediately following the worksheet.

EXERCISE 4: **INTERESTS AND TALENTS**

1. Think of 3-5 moments in your life that could be described as "blissful"; moments when you felt as if you were doing or being what you were meant to do or be, fulfilling your intended purpose. Each may have been a peak experience which made you feel "high," or any poignant moment in which you truly felt you were being yourself. The moments need not pertain to employment, but could be any experience at all.

2. Write a line or two summarizing each experience at the heading. Then, in the space remaining, detail each experience by writing the story and sharing images and thoughts connected with it.

Moment of Bliss #1:

Moment of Bliss #2:

Moment of Bliss #3:

Moment of Bliss #4:

Moment of Bliss #5:

3.   Now examine each moment of Bliss to find what it has to teach you about yourself -- namely, your interests and talents. They may be stated directly, or implied. This requires some careful thought. A partner, perhaps an expressive therapist, may help you see things you might otherwise have blinders to.

Moment of Bliss	Interests Implied	Talents Implied
#1		
#2		
#3		
#4		
#5		

Here is an example to review:

Moment of Bliss #1 (**EXAMPLE 3**): *Feeling Good in the Wood*

The most blissful moment I remember happened when I was only ten years old. It started out like an ordinary day -- but it was gorgeous spring weather, and I was feeling really good. I packed a lunch for myself, took off to the woods next to my house, and after walking a long way, I climbed a tree and sang with the birds at the top of my lungs (No one could hear me -- I was too deep in the woods). It was a song I made up, and I sounded pretty good, too! Then I jumped down and spun around and around under the sun. I dropped on to my back and tried to find animals in the clouds. I talked to God and told my dreams -- what were they? I think I said something about making a difference in the world. I can't believe how optimistic I was about life!

Examining this example, I am reminded at how magical youth can be for many of us. Anything seems possible. Sometimes if people can't recall blissful moments, I refer them to childhood to see if any useful images emerge.

But just what do we learn about *this* young girl in this single example? I will list a few items, in consecutive order rather than order of importance, here:

- This is someone who is clearly drawn to and/or nourished by the outdoors.

- She is resourceful and possesses an independent spirit (retreated to the woods alone, packed her own lunch).

- She very likely has some musical talent as a singer, and she is creative as well (made up her own song).

- She appears to be more introverted than extroverted (relieved that no one can hear her singing, enjoying her own company, basking in the solitude).

- This is also a spiritual person with a calling, a mission, a lofty and worthy purpose. (She dreams of making a difference in the world.)

- She recalls this event with great nostalgia; we wonder if she has lost touch with her youthful, ambitious spirit.

In summary, we can deduce from these notes that, with respect to her talents, the woman probably has some musical ability (we usually love what we are good at). She is resourceful, able to manage tasks independently, and quick to show initiative. She appears to be strongly influenced by her environment, and she has revealed some interests here as well (the outdoors, music, spirituality). She strikes me as being a high achiever.

Letting Images Emerge

There is wisdom in dreams, daydreams as well as night dreams, and unless we pursue them directly, courageously and imaginatively, we may never decipher them and we will certainly never realize them.

"Allowing an image to emerge" is McAuliffe's third stage in the career exploration process (1993, p. 36), after "acknowledging dissonant voices" and "pausing to assess." An image or images of self fulfillment, of a "dream job," may emerge spontaneously, if we are open to the arrival and feel worthy to dream. Some of the exercises in this book might help to coax them out. They may be called forth as well through guided imagery.

Following is a guided imagery text which has been useful to me in workshops. Like most guided imagery, it works best when spoken *very* slowly in a clear and calm voice, over soft music or a very soft drumbeat. The background sound creates a holding environment which helps to contain and preserve the sacredness of the space, making it "safer" for images to emerge. I believe it is helpful, too, for the facilitator to keep his or her intuitive abilities sharp and to *ad lib* on the basic script based on this intuition, in order to respond more effectively to the needs of the group or the individual at the time.

Following the guided imagery, I allow plenty of time for people to record their impressions in visual images, adding words if they seem appropriate.

EXERCISE 5: **MAGIC CARPET RIDE**

Find a comfortable place and position, preferably
lying on your back or sitting in a manner which
allows you to relax, and follow the instructions of the
guided imagery facilitator, as follows. Be sure to
assume a *receptive* posture. Prepare for mystery,
surprise, confusion. Don't try to "make" images;
rather, let them reveal themselves to you. Approach
the process with a childlike interest, curiosity, and
openness. Be open to *whatever* comes and whatever
it has to teach.

Guided Imagery Text:

*Close your eyes, so that you can open your mind's eye to the
imaginal space that surrounds you. Take one or two deep
breaths through your nose, exhaling slowly, feeling the
breathing in and out of air as one continuous motion...*

*As you begin to relax, attend to any parts of your body which
might be holding tension. Find those places, and systematically
tense them and release, relaxing with the release of the tension.
Begin with your toes. Find the tension. Tense your muscles,
hold and release. Move to your calves, and your thighs. Feel
the tension in your abdomen, your diaphragm. Tense, hold,
and release. Find any tension that your fingers or hands might
be holding. Clench your fists, your forearms; hold, and release.
Find the tension in your shoulders and your neck. Tense, hold,
and release. Find the tension in your face -- your forehead,
your eyes. Tense, hold, release, and breathe...*
*Now feel along your back as the fibers of a magic carpet begin
to weave themselves beneath you. Notice the texture and feel
of the fibers, and watch as the colors begin to reveal*

themselves. (Remember, you are seeing with your mind's eye, so there is no need to move your head.) Know that the carpet forming beneath you is a magic carpet, strong and fully able to hold your weight regardless of the density and texture of the fibers. Take some time to notice the carpet in all its glorious detail -- the colors, textures, shapes, designs...

As you lie on the floor, watch with your mind's eye as a tiny spot of sunlight opens in the ceiling above you -- slowing opening, little by little, as the ceiling dissolves. In time the walls, too, begin to dissolve around you. Finally, even the floor dissolves away, and you are left suspended by the strength of the carpet, which begins to tremble, ready to rise and take you on a journey to your future...

Enjoy the ride as the carpet rises above the building, over the city or town or countryside from whence you began. Note the sights below as you travel from this place to a place five years into your future. Pay close attention to where the carpet is taking you--notice the speed with which you are traveling, the distance traveled and the geography of the landscape...

After a time, you will experience a sensation of slowly spiraling downward. You may not be able to see the ground clearly, but you will know when you have landed. Then, feel a new floor forming beneath you, and walls coming up around you, and a ceiling forming above you, putting itself all together in the same manner in which your former shelter dissembled itself...

When the space around you has become fully assembled, and you feel ready, bring your attention to two doors in the room. One is a door you might recognize. It is the door to your future. Behind it lies the places, people and things which you anticipate in your future, five years from now. The other door is a mysterious one. You didn't expect it. You've no idea what lies behind it. Take some time to regard the exteriors of both doors, for in a few minutes you will be asked to choose one of the doors in order to continue your journey...

When you are ready, get up from your carpet, choose one of the doors in the room, and walk over to it. Take another breath. Open the door. Enter the space behind it.

What sights greet you here? Take in the place with all your senses. Is it warm or cold? What are the smells? What does the floor feel like? Notice any furnishings, items on the walls...

Take in every detail. Walk around and browse. Investigate any objects you find...
Is there a window? If you find one, look out to see what is there...
Are there any people here? Who are they? Talk with them to see if they can tell you more about this place...

Before you leave the place, take one last, sweeping look around you, and promise yourself that you will remember every detail... Then say good-bye, and walk out of the door through which you entered. See your magic carpet lying there, waiting for you. Take your time to lie down again and make yourself comfortable...

And again, like before, watch the tiny spot of light appear in the ceiling above you. Watch the ceiling dissolve, the walls, and finally the floor beneath you. Surrender yourself to the strong carpet as it rises up, up into the sky once again, spiraling into the air, carrying you back along the same path which brought you here...

Before you know it, you will be back in the city, town or countryside from whence you began, lying comfortably on your magic carpet...and then on the floor...

When you are ready, take two more slow, deep breaths, and gradually open your eyes. Find your paper and something to draw with and record your impressions.

When you have finished your magic carpet ride, record your impressions here.

Here is more room to record your impressions from the Magic Carpet Ride.

The most compelling thing about this exercise is the enormous variety of impressions it evokes from people. Each person's individuality shines, and the input of others and their observations greatly enrich the images. My approach to interpreting does not include assigning particular meanings to particular symbols; rather, I let the images speak for themselves and enter into dialog with them, in the tradition of Shaun McNiff (1988) and others.

The intent of this guided imagery, as with all the exercises introduced at this exploratory stage, is to bring forth richness, stir the soup, uncover the many aspects that make us individuals. To imagine and draw, and finally to write — write everything down. Once surrounded by the soup, or swimming in it, you will find that the cream will rise. The most critical aspects, the dominant qualities, will weed themselves out and present themselves. They will demand the most attention. Your job is to grapple with them, to clarify them for yourself and then to put them forward in both written and verbal presentations. A key piece of media is the resumé.

The Art of Resumé Writing

A resumé is a crucial marketing tool for anyone conducting a job search. Many employers require it as a method of application. But even if it is not required, a good resumé offers an opportunity to present an image in the most flattering manner possible. Resumé writing can be a therapeutic process, and it can optimize career success.

People today generally want *more* than a "job." Don't you? Don't you want meaningful and satisfying work that is good for the soul? Don't you want Bliss? You are more likely to achieve this objective by crafting a highly individualized resumé designed to attract *quality* (not quantity) contacts and interviews. This requires abandonment of the traditional, formulaic approach -- i.e., to choose a formula from a book or software program and plug in your data. I approach resumé writing as an art. As a "resumé artist," to coin a term, I sift through the variety of material and images gleaned from self exploratory processes, introspection, and dialog. I allow dominant qualities to emerge, and I engage the creative process so that I may **clearly and concisely present an image which effectively conveys the unique essence of a person.** The material is shaped with whatever format and text best express a person's qualities.

A highly individualized resumé stands out from the cookie-cutter variety and leaves a strong and memorable impression. No two finished products are exactly alike, just as no two individuals are exactly alike. There is a natural attraction to a resumé that accurately reflects a person. People whose interests match your own will have the strongest attraction to your resume.

Realize here that when you narrow our focus, you also necessarily *narrow your options.* Therefore, not *everyone* will feel the same degree of attraction to your resumé or fully appreciate your style or your unique blend of talents. But remember, the objective is quality, not quantity. If you are like most people, **you only need *one* job, and it might as well be the *right* job**!

I am reminded of an artistically inclined individual who chose to locate his text flush to the right of the page

---

EXAMPLE 4

I Needa Job   (555) 555-5555
422 Stagecoach Avenue
San Antonio, Texas 02222

Profile   Capable, well-rounded and easygoing individual
                          with keen attention to detail and desire to learn.

                          Able to conceive and translate mental images
                                                    into concrete forms.

                          Imaginative approach to problem-solving.

                          Accustomed to working with minimal supervision.

Experience   ***Kitchen Cabinet Maker***, 10/93 - present.
                                          Kitchen Makers, San Antonio
                     Consult on cabinet design and build all custom cabinets.
                                                    Read blueprints and plans.

                                                                  etc.. . .

(see the fictionalized example, above).*** He found that "artsy" friends loved the resumé. However, he encountered one person who hated it. When I inquired about that person, he shared that he had little in common with the gentleman, who was a "linear-minded," conservative fellow who found the resumé "just too hard to read." Not surprisingly, the man was not a person with whom my client could see himself working.

It is important to mention here that some minimal standard must be adhered to in order to make resumé accessible to people: make them as easy to take in as possible while still maintaining individuality. Resumés must be neatly printed on resumé-quality paper, with no errors or misspellings, and no more than one page in length. Beyond this, there is a great deal of room to be creative.

In order to fully and accurately convey who you are, on paper as well as in person, I encourage you to stick your neck out and take stands on issues that are important to you -- to move beyond a mere listing of sterile tasks and abilities and to let your personality shine through. You can get a lot of mileage from moving beyond "safe" generalizations, like "I like to work with people" (which is tantamount to saying nothing at all) and toward more revealing and descriptive statements. One can reveal much more with a description like, "I bring humor and compassion to my nursing practice, and I am a thorough

---

***I am reluctant to share specific examples of resumés, because I do not wish to encourage the use of examples as models or new formulas to copy. However, I will include a few examples and excerpts to illustrate some points.

and imaginative trainer." Such a statement could cause an employer to lose interest in an applicant if that *employer's* goal is to hire a no-nonsense, regimented nurse to work in an understaffed unit, in which sticking-to-the-script (as opposed to having imagination) are valued in in-service trainers. Neither set of values or priorities is bad, but they are different, and in my view there is no sense in casting lines in places where the catch may be a bad fit.

The guiding principle I use in deciding what to include on a resumé is this: **What defines this person?** Focusing upon your talents and interests is a slightly different twist from the more traditional approach of focusing upon what one imagines is important to an *employer.* The need to reframe this approach is a consequence of the changing nature of the job market, which requires an increased reliance on oneself versus reliance upon an employer, as discussed in the section on re-imagining the game.

This principle guides not only the choice of *content*, but also the way the content is presented; the *style.* The artistic style helps to shape the emotional impact of the resumé. Why does this matter? It is my contention, regardless of how objective or logical people may try to be, that for most employers **hiring is an emotional decision.** People hire people, not pieces of paper or abstract lists of skills, and they hire people whom they imagine they will *like* and with whom they feel comfortable. If someone likes you enough, he or she will find a way to justify the hiring if they need to on paper.

The intense period of introspection and the process of articulating talents and interests in a resumé has clear therapeutic effects. Increased self awareness is an important byproduct, and with it comes a heightened confidence and optimism for realizing goals. Both are necessary for negotiating in today's job market, where self reliance is required, as is the ability to envision niches amidst the ever-changing scenery.

It has been my experience that the qualities of self awareness, confidence and optimism, which the resumé writing process can nurture, are even more important to an effective job search than the resumé itself. I remember working with a woman I'll call Maggie. During our initial consultation, she shared that she had really wanted to leave her current job for a couple of years, but she had never put much effort into the search. After her resumé was completed, I phoned her to arrange for her to pick up the finished copy. Excitedly, she shared that she had landed a new job that very day! Bolstered and rejuvenated by the resumé writing *process*, and armed with a clearer sense of herself and her skills, she had called on a company to inquire about a particular opening and was offered a position right over the phone.

Because effective resumé writing requires artistic talents as well as technical skills, and because another person can often bring a fresh and unbiased perspective on an individual's traits, there is no shame in seeking professional help from a resumé artist. To be sure, most people can fill in the blanks of an application form; this is a purely technical task. But not everyone can bring an artist's intuition to the crafting of a resumé -- just as it would be a rare C.E.O. who would prepare his own corporate marketing materials. (C.E.O.s routinely hire artists and consultants for the task, while of course remaining involved in the process by describing the image they wish to have conveyed.) A resumé artist can also help you to see and appreciate talents and uncover interests you may not have had the courage to confront.

Resumé Anatomy

A resumé need not correspond to any particular format, so job seekers are at liberty to include whatever information seems most relevant, and to downplay or even omit certain items and highlight others. But the resumé *does* need to summarize in a concise manner any and all information pertinent to your ability, qualifications and working style. In other words, it needs to answer the question: "Who are you, and why should I hire you?" There are essentially two parts to a resumé required to answer these basic questions.

The Profile. First, a *profile*, or a summary of qualifications and skills, **summarizes the essence of a person,** including the dominant qualities that emerge from material pulled from self awareness exercises and in dialog with a resumé artist. Brevity is important here, and bulleted items are the easiest to read quickly. Studies in perception have shown that the human brain can easily hold no more than five bits of data at a time; this is a rough guideline I use for how many items to include on a profile, though it is not set in stone.

The Proof. Once the essence is summarized, the remainder of the resumé must set about the task of **offering the evidence to *support* the statements made in the profile.** This "proof" can be summarized in a variety of sections. The *order* in which you list your proof depends upon what you wish to emphasize more or less, but for the most part the sections will include the following:

- *employment* or work history.
- *education and training.*

- *memberships and professional affiliations.*
- any other pertinent information; e.g., community service, internship experience, volunteer work, and so forth.

The names, addresses and phone numbers of *references*, who are the people who can vouch for your qualities, are generally not listed on the resumé itself. However, most resumés add a line stating that they can be furnished upon request. This final statement is somewhat optional, since it does not provide any particular informative data; however, I usually include it as it serves the function of offering a cue to the reader that the resumé is ended.

The Objective. "So what about an *objective?*" I often hear this question as a worried inquiry, sometimes with a gasp. For it is a fact that many, many resumés begin with a bold announcement of an objective. Here is my unwavering opinion on the subject: Objectives are important to state and be clear about -- but they belong in a cover letter, not on a resumé. When I see them on resumés, they typically are written in such a general fashion that they lack meaning (e.g., "I am seeking a job that will utilize my skills and give me opportunities to advance."), or else they are written so specifically that they effectively rule out golden opportunities that a person has not yet imagined. Especially in today's market, with jobs and entire industries becoming obsolete every day, it is important to remain flexible to the variety of opportunities which can arise. Besides, why waste *prime space* on a resumé with ambiguous statements?

Let's return to the second main part of the resumé, information required to "prove" or support one's profile. It is important to be selective here, but I have found it most valuable to first collect *all* the data, and then select the most pertinent to include. The resumé worksheet which begins on the following page is a helpful tool for collecting this data.

Many people have the misconception that if they have more than one major interest or area of talent, they need to create more than one resumé to address each area, so that different resumés can be used for different positions. In a wholeness-based approach to resumé writing, the objective is to convey the essence of a person and *all* of his or her dominant qualities in order to give the reader a complete image of what that person wishes to offer in a job. This requires leaving "no stone unturned," and no major piece omitted. One resumé is enough. The art lies in conveying the package with a sense of wholeness.

EXERCISE 6: **Data Collection Worksheet**

This is not a resumé outline, but rather a vehicle to aid in the collection of information. For the finished resumé, some data will of course need to be cut, and most will be rearranged to reflect individual strengths.

While filling in the blanks, keep in mind that the process of writing a resumé is itself of value, because it helps to inventory abilities and build confidence. It also provides information for interviews and serves as a memory-jogger. Be thorough and print clearly.

PART I. IDENTIFYING INFORMATION

Name_____

Credentials [degree, license]_____

Address_____ Apt._____

City/State/Zip_____

Home Phone_____ Work Phone_____

E-mail_____

Other (cell phone, website, etc.)_____

Best time/method to contact_____

PART II. EDUCATION

Highest degree attained_____ Month/Year_____

School/City_____

Other_____ Month/Year_____

School/City_____

Other_____ Month/Year_____

School/City_____

List other schooling or training, including workshops, seminars, and in service training below and/or on additional paper.

_____

_____

PART III. EMPLOYMENT [most recent first]

Job #1 [title]_____ Dates employed_____

Company/Firm_____

Supervisor_____

City/State_____

For the following section on "duties," see the "Action Words" list that follows this worksheet. Get in the habit of using action words to describe duties and achievements. Begin every phrase with an action verb, then follow with a subject. (Examples: "Handled mail." "Counseled people with disabilities." "Loaded and unloaded inventory." "Negotiated contracts.")

Sentences may be expanded to more fully reflect strengths, but be as concise as possible. (Examples: "Designed an outreach program to expand services." "Increased annual sales by 20%." "Set up database for tracking customers.") When describing a current job, use the present tense. (Examples: "Maintain books." "Supervise 25 support staff.")

Duties_____

_____

_____

_____

_____

_____

Circle: (part-time) (full-time) (internship) (volunteer)

Job #2_____ Dates employed_____

Company/Firm_____

Supervisor_____

City/State_____

Duties_____

_____

_____

_____

_____

_____

Circle: (part-time) (full-time) (internship) (volunteer)

Job #3_____ Dates employed_____

Company/Firm_____

Supervisor_____

City/State_____

Duties_____

_____

_____

_____

_____

Circle: (part-time) (full-time) (internship) (volunteer)

Job #4_____ Dates employed_____

Company/Firm_____

Supervisor_____

City/State_____

Duties_____

_____

_____

_____

_____

_____

Circle: (part-time) (full-time) (internship) (volunteer)

Job #5_____ Dates employed_____

Company/Firm_____

Supervisor_____

City/State_____

Duties_____

_____

_____

_____

_____

Circle: (part-time) (full-time) (internship) (volunteer)

PART IV. PROFESSIONAL MEMBERSHIPS

Position held, if any_____Dates_____

Organization_____

Description of duties or achievements:_____

_____

_____

_____

Position held, if any_____Dates_____

Organization_____

Description of duties or achievements:_____

_____

_____

_____

Position held, if any_____Dates_____

Organization_____

Description of duties or achievements:_____

_____

_____

_____

PART V. REFERENCES

References need to be readily available when requested. Call people who know your work, and notify them *before* you share their names with anyone. Recent supervisors are best; teachers, colleagues or co-workers are okay, and for some industries, customers may provide useful testimonials. Only use a "personal" reference, or friend, as a last resort. Supervisors can vouch for your character as well as friends. Never use relatives.

Remember too that people move away, and they also forget. Ask your references *now* to write a letter of recommendation to pass on to future prospective employers. Make several copies and keep them on hand to send or deliver when requested.

Reference #1 [name]_____

Relationship [supervisor, teacher,etc.]_____

Title_____Affiliation [firm/school]_____

Address_____ Apt._____

City/State/Zip_____

Reference #2 _____

Relationship_____

Title_____Affiliation_____

Address_____ Apt._____

City/State/Zip_____

Reference #3 _____

Relationship_____

Title_____Affiliation_____

Address_____ Apt._____

City/State/Zip_____

PART VI. OTHER SPECIAL TALENTS

  Typing. Words per minute:_____

  Computer hardware and peripherals:_____
  _____

  Computer software and operating systems:_____
  _____

  Languages:_____

  Machines operated:_____

  Publications and writings:_____
  _____
  _____

  Other special attributes (e.g., photographic memory,
  knowledge of medical terminology, ability to meet
  deadlines, excellent phone manner, etc.):_____
  _____
  _____
  _____

ADDENDUM. ACTION WORDS

achieved	created	followed	memorized	reproduced
accepted	cut	formulated	mentored	resolved
acted	dealt with	found	met	responded
addressed	debated	founded	modeled	retained
adjusted	decided	gained	monitored	retrained
advised	defined	gathered	motivated	retrieved
aided	delivered	gave	negotiated	reviewed
allocated	designed	generated	nursed	scheduled
anticipated	detected	graphed	nurtured	screened
applied	determined	guided	observed	searched
appraised	developed	handled	obtained	selected
arranged	devised	helped	operated	serviced
assembled	diagnosed	hired	ordered	set up
assessed	directed	hosted	organized	sketched
attained	discovered	identified	persuaded	simplified
balanced	dispatched	illustrated	painted	sold
briefed	displayed	imagined	performed	solved
brought	distributed	improved	placed	sorted
budgeted	drafted	improvised	planned	sought
built	drew	increased	played	specialized
calculated	drove	influenced	possessed	spoke
cared for	duplicated	initiated	posted	studied
carried	edited	inspected	prepared	summarized
chaired	eliminated	inspired	prescribed	supplied
charted	empathized	instituted	presented	surveyed
checked	emphasized	instructed	produced	taught
clarified	employed	interviewed	promoted	tended
classified	encouraged	intuited	proofread	tested
cleaned	enforced	invented	protected	took
coached	enjoyed	inventoried	publicized	trained
collaborated	entered	investigated	purchased	transcribed
collated	estimated	judged	raised	traveled
collected	exceeded	kept	read	treated
completed	excelled	learned	received	tutored
conceived	executed	led	recognized	understood
conducted	expanded	lifted	recorded	updated
confronted	expressed	listened	recruited	upgraded
conserved	extracted	loaded	redesigned	used
contacted	facilitated	made	reduced	utilized
copied	farmed	maintained	referred	weighed
corrected	figured	managed	renewed	won
counseled	filed	mapped	repaired	worked
counted	focused	mastered	reported	wrote

A person I'll call David came to me seeking career counseling and brought with him a two-page resumé which reflected only one dimension of his background, his sales experience. He began with a general objective which consumed about an eighth of the page, listed a few sales skills, and summarized a few sales jobs from his employment history. It was typical of the resumés I see.

David had two other major areas of interest which were nowhere reflected in his resume. One of his omissions was his "secret life" as a musician. He was a consummate and accomplished guitarist, who practiced his instrument for several hours a day and studied with some of the finest musicians in his city; but he had never performed publicly. The other omission was a love for the restaurant industry. The bulk of *this* experience dated back to his college days.

First of all, I insisted that David, for homework, arrange to perform at an open mike session in his city. (The first priority, in my view, was to feed this neglected passion.) Then, I worked on introducing some wholeness to David's resumé. A modified excerpt appears on the following page.

Once we finished the resumé, we knew that one of three responses could be expected from potential employers looking to hire for a sales position:

- One reader might hate the resumé and respond with, "What do I care that he's a musician?" Given David's passion and insecurity about performing, a derisive attitude was the last thing he needed.

- A second reader might not have any particular interest in musical skills or restaurant knowledge, but may find the applicant more *interesting* and well-rounded, and may even share a passion for music that could enable a point of mutual appreciation beyond the sales position in question.

• A third might actually *seek* an applicant with all David's talents. (Imagine that!)

Fortunately for David, within a matter of a few weeks he landed something of a "dream job," an account executive supervising sales for a growing chain of restaurant/night clubs, in which live entertainment was a major part of the fare. In this position, *all* his skills and interests mattered. He was perfectly suited to the work.

You may wonder what happened with David's initial "homework." Because the territory was untried, we had no idea what taking the risk to perform might lead to. Like many, he simply needed to honor and give voice to his passion, so that he could better understand what it was about. When we *stifle* a passion, our awareness of what it really means to us can become clouded or distorted. For David, finding time to perform did not require him to give up other parts of his life for a "life on the road." On the contrary, there exist a number of ways that his talent can enrich his life and the lives of others without being all-consuming. And I trust that it has.

EXAMPLE 5: DAVID, AFTER

DAVID RESUMÉ
454 Bridge Avenue   Yarmouth, New Hampshire 55555   (555) 555-5555

- Disciplined, versatile and self directed high achiever.
- Outstanding track record in sales and management.
- Well developed consultative selling, closing and communication skills.
- Knowledge and experience in all phases of the restaurant industry.
- Effective and creative planner with an eye for cost reduction strategies.
- Versatile guitarist with special skills and interest in jazz and jazz blues.

EMPLOYMENT
District Sales Manager, 6/92 - 10/93
Data Is Us, Harvard Satellite Office, New Hampshire
Advanced from temporary position in finance. Engaged in all aspects of prospecting, sales and closing.

Salesperson (twice rated #2 in company), 10-91 - 5/92
Fox Industries, Portland, Maine
Handled proposals, demonstrations, closings. Sold over $100K in 3 months.

District Salesperson [...]

Function Coordinator, 12/86 - 8/90
Famous Restaurant, San Diego, California
Performed sales and staffing responsibilities. Organized large functions. Transferred to Chicago to open a premier steakhouse. Assisted new management in scheduling and training staff.

General Manager...[another famous restaurant...]

EDUCATION
Berklee College of Music, Boston, Massachusetts, 6/79 - 5/81
Completed studies in arranging, theory, harmony and professional film scoring.

Accounting course, State University, 1978

REFERENCES furnished upon request.

Artistic Presentation and Style

Whenever I do resumé writing workshops I like to use an exercise in which I quickly walk around the room passing out sample resumés. As soon as I complete my circle, I retrace my steps and pick each sample up again. Then I ask people to jot down whatever impressions come to mind about the resumés they'd only briefly encountered. I remind them that a prospective employer will form an initial impression of their resumés in only a few seconds, and this impression will determine whether they read on. What I don't tell them is that many of the resumés they have scanned are "before and after" resumés of the same people. The exercise is an excellent way to bring home to people the importance of making use of the artistic tools we have available to us to emphasize or de-emphasize items and also to impart styles and suggest visual images consistent with our personalities.

You can get a sense of the impact of the exercise by glancing at the two examples on the next two pages. What stands out to most people in the first example are the capitalized *headings*. This does the job candidate no good at all. The second sample resumé, using size, bold type, and more sensible positioning, better ensures that the person's *name* will be remembered, highlights her *strengths* right off the bat, and eliminates or downplays the less important text. Both examples fit on a single page, but look how much more the second example tells us about Rosalind. As far a content goes, we learn about her varied interests, her working style, and her involvement in her community. The unique typeface used with her name better reflects her personality, with a touch of flair we'd have no notion of in the first example. Which version would make a stronger impression on *you*?

EXAMPLE 6: ROSALIND, BEFORE

Rosalind T. Goldstein
17 Tulip Lane
Fictionaltown, CH 55555
(555) 555-5555

OBJECTIVE: FULL-TIME employment, utilizing my previous experience of dealing with people.

EDUCATION: Fictional School of Dental Nursing

EXPERIENCE: Farley Corporation D.B.A. Helping Others (June 1, 1992 to present)

Office Manager/Patient Benefits Coordinator:

* answering phone calls
* greeting clients
* maintaining copies of clinician schedules
* ascertaining insurance benefits and confirming benefits
* fielding client questions Re: billing and benefits
* keeping medical records accessible and proper order
* word processing: Microsoft Word
* responsible for office upkeep and supplies

HELPING OTHERS, INC., (1982-1991)

Receptionist/Medical Billing/Data Entry

REFERENCES: Available upon request

EXAMPLE 7: ROSALIND, AFTER

Rosalind T. Goldstein
17 Tulip Lane   Office: (555) 444-4444
Fictionaltown, CH 55555   Home: (555) 555-5555

- Warm, personable and conscientious self-starter with seasoned skills in **office management, fund-raising** and **event planning/coordination.**
- Very strong people skills; able to maintain poise and rapport even when dealing with crises, "difficult" clients, children and collections problems.
- Familiar with operation of mental health and insurance agencies and small businesses.
- Long-standing interest in music and the arts.
- Computer literate; skilled in Microsoft Word, medical billing software.

Professional Experience

Office Manager/Patient Benefits Coordinator, 1992 - present
Farley Corporation, D/B/A Helping Others, Fictionaltown
Manage office. Handle special billing problems. Prepare reports, correspondence. Put clients at ease for therapy appointments. Organize staff parties. Redecorated the office.

Receptionist/Medical Billing/Data Entry, 1982 - 1991
Helping Others, Inc., Fictionaltown
Greeted clients. Screened/referred callers. Handled intakes and billing.

Manager/Bookkeeper, Ace Shoes, Metropolis, 1978 - 1982
Purchased inventory. Managed sales, personnel and bookkeeping.

Community Service

Parent Teacher Organization (PTO)
Active member/spokesperson for 10 years. Served as President and Vice President. Led successful fundraiser to build playground and school addition.

School Committee and Youth Commission, Fiction Temple
Co-chaired 25th Anniversary Art Show in 1986; participated in art show committees in prior years (solicited donations, located artists, purchased/hung art, prepared hall.)

Education

Dental Assistant certificate, Fictional School of Dental Nursing
Completed 1-year certificate training and 7 years employment as dental assistant.

References **furnished upon request.**

Symbols, visual images and even watermarks can be incorporated in *subtle,* even subliminal, ways to help reflect the person portrayed. Jane (below) worked with contractors in the home building industry. One subtle way in which we illustrated her resumé was to use small house shapes (pentagons) for bullets in her profile.

EXAMPLE 8: RESUMÉ GRAPHICS

Jane Doe
111 Brookside, Keene, New York 55555
(555) 555-5555

- Creative, straightforward and capable sale professional.
- Organized and detail oriented, with superb problem solving skills.
- Quick learner with demonstrated initiative and resourcefulness.
- Computer literate; familiar with CAD and 20/20.
- Extensively trained, with vast product knowledge and skills in design strategies in contracting and home remodeling.

etc...

I have seen many more dramatic touches. As a person in charge of hiring, I remember receiving a large, three-fold resumé, with a full-size photograph of the person applying for the job on the front. It was a bit of a turn-off for me personally, but I can leave room for the possibility that someone else might have been sold. To the individual's credit, he did make an impression, and I have never forgotten that resumé. The main point is to include *what suits the individual* and best reflects the person. Moreover, as resumé writers, we need to take care that the artistic styles we use do reflect the *individuals* portrayed, and not our *own* personal styles.

There is much that can be done with choices of typeface, too. With one individual, I incorporated an ornate, flowery typeface (*Sara Goodnature*) into many of her headings. Many writers would never think of using this typeface; indeed, it was a rare choice even for me, since it takes so much time to read. But Sara is a *person who takes time*. She is a patient and intuitive psychotherapist with a strong Eastern influence, who works at a measured pace and gives her clients lots of room to explore and grow. A bold, Helvetica typeface would have created a completely different and inaccurate impression.

Margaret's resumé, which appears on the following page, conveys a different impression, but one well-suited to her personality. Margaret is a direct person with simple interests, whose sense of identity focuses primarily on her career.

Incidentally, this is also a mature person who wished to downplay her age and did so by listing her dates worked in small type, positioned in a place of minimal emphasis. Notice also how she takes a string of temporary positions and gives them a sense of wholeness by grouping them in the first employment section.

Finally, a word about paper. Resumés deserve to be printed on resumé quality paper; that means at least a twenty-five pound weight. The color, if any, should be pale enough so that the print will stand out easily and copy well. I recommend against a pure, untextured white, since the paper has no chance to stand out against the myriad of other white papers on a typical person's desk. An off-white or cream is a fine, conservative choice. I have also seen tasteful textures, speckled papers, and pale colors.

EXAMPLE 9: MARGARET, AFTER

Margaret E. Resume
114 Summer Street
Fictiontown, Massachusetts 55555
(555) 555-5555

SUMMARY OF QUALIFICATIONS

Energetic and capable business professional with diverse skills.
Smart, personable and accountable for own work.
Rarely absent, with high level of company loyalty.
Relates easily with people, honestly and directly.
Notary Public in seventh term.
Types 50 wpm; some word processing experience.
Prefers part-time position, no weekends.

EMPLOYMENT

Bookkeeper, Office Manager and **Salesperson**, 1990 - present
Various locations in Central Massachusetts
Assumed a variety of responsibilities in temporary, part-time and freelance capacity. Maintained books, handled payroll and performed routine office functions. Prepared quotes for an electrician. Handled books for a local restaurant. Sold products for a plastic resins company.

Purchasing Agent, 1955 - 1990
Papa's Plastics, Inc., Greenfield, Massachusetts
Advanced in the company from the position of Assistant Purchasing Agent and Receptionist. Purchased all materials pertaining to production. Approved invoices and purchase orders. Ensured timely delivery of materials. Monitored activities in the warehouse and maintained contact with employees in order to respond to their special needs or requests. Prepared financial reports. Handled all company airline and hotel reservations. Assumed accounts payable duties as needed (posted billings, wrote checks, reconciled journals). Operated switchboard.

EDUCATION

Basic Income Tax Preparation (6 mos + internship), H&R Block
Traffic Management and Freight Rate (2 semesters), City Junior College
High School graduate

REFERENCES furnished upon request.

The psychology of color tells us that hue has its own influence on readers; navy blue, for example, reminds us of uniforms and inspires respect. Rose is a warm, feminine color. Greens and browns are reminiscent of nature. I could go on; however, I have found that when people simply select what most attracts them, those colors and textures will naturally fit and reflect their personal styles.

"But I Have No Skills!"

So what of the person who "has no skills"? You might guess that this is my pet peeve. There is no such thing as a person with no skills! I like to illustrate this fact by describing a young man I'll call Frankie Young. When I knew him, I was doing some work at a program for disadvantaged youth in Fitchburg, Massachusetts. At the time, Massachusetts had the highest unemployment rate in the country, and Fitchburg had the highest unemployment rate in the state. Frankie lived in the poorest part of the city, where drug dealing appeared to be the prominent industry, and most of the people lived in a pre-welfare reform culture which lacked the work ethic with which I feel fortunate to have grown up. None of Frankie's friends had ever had jobs, and most of their single parents had never worked either. But -- lo and behold -- Frankie had a job, and a bright future as well. A modified version of the resumé we prepared appears above. Frankie is proof that no one is a hopeless case.

EXAMPLE 10

Frankie Young
800 Gangland Street, 2nd Floor
Fitchburg, Massachusetts 01420
(555) 555-5555

Profile
- Well-rounded, responsible worker with good work habits.
- Interested in exploring a career in law enforcement.
- Technical training in construction, electricity, auto mechanics, welding and plumbing.
- Bilingual in English and Spanish.

Experience

Carpenter Helper, 7/93 - present
YoungBuilders Program, Fitchburg, Massachusetts
Work on renovations and remodeling projects, including demolition and bath construction. Maintain clean work site. Work year-round; part-time during the school year and full-time during summer months.

Short-Order Cook (part-time), 1992
FastFood Restaurant, Fitchburg, Massachusetts

Maintenance Worker, Summer 1991
City School, Fitchburg, Massachusetts
Cleaned classrooms. Polished floors. Maintained grounds. Did indoor/outdoor painting. Washed windows.

General Technician, Summer 1990
Vocational Technical School
Performed various technical tasks while receiving on-the-job training in auto body, auto mechanics, woodworking, welding and plumbing.

Education

High School Diploma, anticipated 6/95
City High School

References

furnished upon request.

Accompaniments to the Resumé

To optimize career success, once you put together a strong resumé, you will need to gather a portfolio of accompaniments that may include some or all of the following:

- a nicely typed list of references.
- three or more letters of recommendation.
- work samples and/or writing samples.
- transcripts, certificates, licenses, or lists of seminars completed.
- other addenda detailing particular achievements.
- cover letters.

Samples of various resume accompaniments follow.

EXAMPLE 11: SAMPLE REFERENCE SHEET

References of Joe Resume

Harry S. Boss, M.B.A.	Current Supervisor
Chief Executive Officer	(111) 111-1111
Ace Company	
432 Fictional Street	
Hobunk, Alaska 55555	
Julia Morrison, Director	Former Supervisor
National Museum of Paraphernalia	(222) 222-2222
199 North Main Street	
Washington, DC 00000	
Merilee Mustardface	Fomer Supervisor
Highland Park Community College	(333P 333-3333
Arlington, Virginia 33333	

References. Note in the sample reference sheet on the previous page that you will generally need *three* references (a standard required number), and that you should list not only the name of each reference, but also the person's title, address, telephone number, and relationship to you. Having this document handy (printed on identical paper and in a similar style to your resume) makes a more professional impression and makes hiring you easier for the employer.

If you have not worked recently, you may use a "character reference" (someone who does not necessarily know your work but can vouch for your character, usually a professional friend -- minister, accountant, lawyer, doctor). This practice is most common among young adults or others with little or no work experience. But try not to use more than one character reference. It is important to use people who *know your work.* (They can vouch for your character, too!) Never use relatives.

Letters of Recommendation. Letters of recommendation are valuable for a variety of reasons:
- They can detail your strengths precisely.
- You know exactly what they say.
- They may save an interviewer from making phone calls on references.
- They can record work that you did for someone who may no longer be available by phone, or at all.

Letters of recommendation need not correspond precisely with your reference list. They should always be presented on the author's letterhead -- not yours. For your portfolio, a photocopy of the original letter is fine.

Don't be afraid to help someone write your letter of

recommendation. You know better than anyone else all the wonderful work you have done in the past, and you can remind a former employer of those things.

A sample letter of recommendation appears below.

EXAMPLE 12:
SAMPLE LETTER OF RECOMMENDATION

AMALGAMATED TIRE, INC.

June 5, 1997

To whom it may concern:

I have known Susie Resume for the past eight years. During that time, I have supervised her in our sales division.

Ms. Resume's excellent sales record speaks for itself. She was one of our top three salespersons, earning many company awards for exceeding sales goals. Always courteous and helpful with customers, she was able to quickly establish rapport and was well liked. She was easy to supervise, showing initiative when appropriate and taking criticism well. She also supervised two junior sales representatives and handled this responsibility well and conscientiously.

Ms. Resume's presence will be missed as she pursues other areas of interest. Her contributions to this company have been substantial, and I recommend her for employment without reservation.

Sincerely,

Harry Williams
Harry Williams, Manager

Cover Letters. The best cover letter is tailored to a particular job or lead, and the more information you have before writing it, the better. Try to get the name and title of the person in charge of hiring and as much information about the job itself as possible. It's worth a phone call or two to get the information.

A sample cover letter appears on the following page. The body of every cover letter has three basic parts. In the first paragraph of the body of the letter, state your intent; that is, answer the question, "Why am I writing?" The second and sometimes third paragraphs allow you to call attention to your resumé, highlighting what you want noticed, and adding any details about your qualifications that may not be included in the resumé. Here you answer the question, "Why should you hire me?" And in the final paragraph, indicate the "next step." The more proactive, the better.

To conclude, once you have your resumé and portfolio in order, you will find it to be useful in several ways. First of all, the process of writing the resumé will have already made you more aware of your gifts and talents and boosted your self esteem and confidence about landing a job. You can then use your resumé as a vehicle for applying for advertised openings or for making inquiries with people who may not be advertising, but with whom you are interested in working.

But before you get too far into the job search, make sure you have a plan. A plan can further narrow your focus and guide you in setting monthly and even daily objectives for yourself as you set about giving substance to the images you have called.

EXAMPLE 13:
SAMPLE COVER LETTER

Susie Resume
18 Hanover Street, Pittsburgh, PA 55555   *(555) 555-5555*

December 14, 1999

John Employer
ABC Technology
123 Alphabet Park
Hancock, Virginia 66666

Dear Mr. Employer:

I am writing to submit my resume in application for the position of **Office Clerk**, which I saw advertised in Sunday's *Gazette*.

I have been a clerical worker for fifteen years. My experience has included handling phones, bookkeeping and light typing, and I have been told that my filing skills are "superb."

I will be calling you on Thursday to ensure that you have received my resume and to see when we might get together to talk more about your needs and my qualifications.

Sincerely,

Susie Resume
Susie Resume

Enclosure: Resume

STEP FOUR:
GIVING SUBSTANCE TO IMAGES

[I want to] make sure that everyone who has a job
wants a job.
-- George Bush, during his first campaign for the presidency

In 1995, I attended an enlightening presentation by futurist Ed Barlow. He spoke convincingly, at length, and with no small measure of passion about the enormous uncertainty the future held. He spoke about rapid advances in technology and observed that fully half of the jobs to be had in this country in the year 2000 did not even exist then. (I believe he was right.) He urged those present not to rest in complacency, but to position ourselves and actively prepare for the future, which was already upon us.

Inevitably, a frustrated executive in attendance offered the plea, "But how can I *plan* in an environment of *uncertainty* like the one you describe?" The plea gave us all pause, including Mr. Barlow, who deferred the question to the latter part of his presentation. He did return to the point, albeit briefly, and suggested an approach of "scanning and evaluating" all that we saw happening around us.

This was certainly an important part of the answer. However, it did not seem to fully satisfy the crowd. I imagined that the executive who had asked the question might have wondered, "What is the point in scanning and evaluating the *present*? I need to anticipate five or more years down the road!" I sensed a general consensus that the problem was a difficult one for which there simply existed no better solution than the one Barlow had given.

But there *is* a more complete answer to the quandary inherent in this line of argument. Scan and evaluate the present, yes. Yet more than this, **we need to fine-tune our sensitivity to and learn to trust our *intuitions* about the future.** These intuitions may be subtle as a feeling of being passionately drawn to a thing, without even understanding why. It is the "follow your Bliss" approach put into action on a day-to-day basis. Every yearning, however great or small, emerges in synchronicity with a corresponding need in the universe. A spiritual self awareness, above all, includes an awareness of one's yearnings, and responding to them leads to spiritual fulfillment.

There is wisdom in gut feelings and in Bliss, and if we trust and follow their calls, manifested in feelings of passion and excitement, the wisdom will be revealed in time. Moreover, this wisdom is a wisdom of the universe, not just of individuals, so that in following Bliss, we not only reap the rewards of personal satisfaction, but we also identify and meet real needs in the world around us. I learned this lesson in my own life.

My career path began at an early age. I had a passion for so many things, and I felt despair when others more experienced than I advised me to "choose one." Specifically, as a young person, I was fascinated by human beings as a study, and passionate about the arts. I loved the arts, sensed their connectedness, and showed talent in many branches of the arts -- music, sculpture, drawing, and creative writing, to name a few.

I began in a traditional music therapy program, which was a partial integration of my interests, but I found it too restrictive. In my second year, I transferred to a more flexible, design-your-own-major program and crafted an integrated curriculum which let me combine a study of the arts and human psychology. Upon concluding my undergraduate degree, I listened to my gut and took a paraprofessional position in an employment and training program for people with epilepsy. I stayed six years, honing both my career counseling and administrative skills, for in time I was asked to direct the national program. With no place further to go in that job, I hungered for an advanced degree. By this time I had learned of a graduate program in psychotherapy which promoted an integrated arts approach, the Expressive Therapies program at Lesley College Graduate School in Cambridge, Massachusetts.

Mind you, I loved the job I was leaving. I was better paid than most of my peers at that time, and the work itself fed a real passion. I looked forward to going to work and felt rewarded at the end of each day. Those looking from the outside in tried to appeal to my "rationality" by advising, "So, why don't you keep your job and study at night; and if you love your work so much, why not get an advanced degree in vocational rehabilitation or career development?"

They meant well, but I had two clear reasons why I could not follow this advice: The options held no spark for me, and I hungered for something different. I could not explain the logic in it, for the reasons burst from my *heart*, not from my intellect. I was called. And in a decision that I thought at the time might very well sever any further connection with this world I had grown to love so much, I quit my job, rented a U-Haul, and moved myself to Massachusetts to rekindle the artist's spirit in me.

The psychotherapeutic training was difficult, emotionally demanding, and exceedingly rewarding. The relationships I forged were precious and lasting. And when I finished, I emerged (to my surprise) not as a "new" person shaped in a new form by the training I had received, but rather as the same person with all the same passions, but with a broader repertoire of skills. As if by magic, the training had become fully integrated into the person I was. I felt the spiritual awareness that I was becoming even more the person I was intended to be. I was not Bob Newhart, the television psychologist, nor was I the psychiatrist from *Ordinary People*, nor was I *Sybil's* therapist as portrayed by Joanne Woodward. These were the images I had carried with me of people working as psychotherapists. No, I was Helen Barba, and I had some important ideas to share about career-life planning, and how pleasantly surprised I was to find that my blend of talents and training had uniquely equipped me to fill a hungry niche in the field. The marriage of talents seems so sensible and clear to me now; but this awareness came only *after* my clinical training was complete, when I decided to establish a private practice. I had something fresh and new to offer this field I loved.

My husband's career path held similar surprises. After years of working successfully in news radio (which he loved) he felt it was time for a change. He took a chance and quit his job to work in his father's plumbing business. He got his journeyman's license while he anguished (just a little) over what he was going to do with the rest of his life. What, after all, did communications and plumbing have in common? He found his perfect niche -- that of national training manager for a large manufacturer of plumbing and heating equipment. He was always an animated trainer and loved entertaining, and with the expertise he acquired in the plumbing and heating product line and the ins-and-outs of installation, he became the perfect candidate for this job. It offered greater exposure and room for advancement as well as greater financial rewards than anything else he had done to date. He was fully in his element in this work.

Following Bliss can impact not only individuals, but also entire industries. Not long ago, I read wisdom in the calls of a number of younger peers in the field of expressive therapies. While teaching second-year graduate students at Lesley College, I became aware of a phenomenon which revealed itself separately to three different students. It was called the "expressive therapy café." I first became aware of the phenomenon as a brainstorm of a student in my thesis seminar. She had left a successful career as a restauranteur to study the expressive therapies. She had a dream of one day creating a dining/therapeutic environment which would be surrounded by art and make available to patrons seductive art materials and opportunities to be creative. At about the same time, I learned of another student who was trying (without much success, as it happened) to get approval to write a thesis on an "expressive therapy café" model. Her thesis instructor was concerned at the time that the material was "not clinical enough"; that is, it did not fit the established paradigm for how people could or should use their talents as expressive therapists. A third student, at the same time, actually *started up* an "expressive therapy café" on campus; it became a meeting place for students to create and share art and also nurture themselves with food and drink in an informal environment.

To my knowledge, none of these students knew each other. Each of them probably felt she had an original idea

-- and each had a passion for the idea. This was Bliss! It is clear to me that the idea was bigger than the sum of the individuals. And it is clear to me that the impulse came as a response to a need in the universe for a nurturing haven and creative outlet for people stressed out with their high-tech, low-touch lives.

Imagine the courage required to forge ahead and blaze a new trail such as this. It would mean creating a new paradigm and finding a way to resolve ethical questions and logistical details the likes of which contemporary psychotherapists have not yet had to face. It would force practitioners in the field of expressive therapy to take a hard look at the way we think about our work, and to shift notions about the diverse ways in which our skills and talents might serve the world.

This scenario is by no means isolated, either. Ed Barlow (1995) points out that most of the growth happening today in the labor market is happening *across* industries. Successful companies are stepping outside familiar territory and into completely new industries to tap into brand new markets.

Some measure of courage is always required when it comes to following Bliss, for not only does it challenge traditions, but it also forces us to step outside established routines in big and small ways, when the rationale may not be clear at all, and often in the absence of support from family and friends. We need to trust that the gains will outweigh the losses in the surrender.

The follow-your-Bliss posture is important not only for the "big decisions." It is important to weigh our passion even as we plan our daily schedules. When we assess what is important to us as we set about writing a five-year plan, for example, we need to be sure that we translate our aspirations into daily tasks. We must make sure that we can find enjoyment every day, and never do anything merely as a means to an end. I have known too many people who have suffered themselves through a formal education with the fantasy that they'd like what came out at the other end -- and instead they continued to be miserable.

Let your own Bliss be the beacon which guides you in your short and long range planning, as well as your moment-to-moment existence.

Preparing for Change:
Goal Setting and Planning

I remember the eagerness with which my bouncing niece anticipated her entry into the first grade. For weeks her grandmother, "Nona," had been telling her of the many adventures which awaited her at "the *big* school." She looked forward with the greatest anticipation to learning to read. Oh, how she wanted to read *all by herself.* Her excitement piqued as she set off on that first day of school. But when Nona greeted her at the end of the day, it was a devastated little girl who met her. "Nona," she exclaimed, incredulously, "I can't read!"

'Lainey did not learn to read overnight, but she *did* learn to read. Change usually does not happen overnight. More often, it requires a conscious commitment followed by careful planning.

Change begins with the courage to *imagine* a goal, and it is significantly empowered by the mere writing down of that goal. I always caution people: Be careful what you wish for; it might come true! In my own life, I am accustomed to writing (and periodically reviewing) a five-year plan, and once I write my intentions down they seem to take on a life of their own. In my last plan, I wrote that I would like to have three children over the course of five years. I had three children in three years -- and a "bonus" before the fifth year came! I also decided that I would very much like to teach in a university. I actually broke that goal down into do-able chunks, to include pursuit of a doctoral degree in addition to several other steps along the way. Almost in spite of my "plan," I found myself on a university faculty within a year of writing that goal -- without having yet acquired or even begun working towards my doctoral degree. I have an acquaintance who tells me he has *never* failed to achieve a goal that he has written down. What a power!

Priorities

Most planning systems begin with goal-setting. I precede the goal-setting with another task: conducting a careful assessment of priorities. This task should follow the completion of the self awareness exercises already presented, so that you may begin with a good sense of your values and dominant qualities.

EXERCISE 7: **PRIORITIZING**

First, make a list of what is most important to you -- say, three to seven priorities. *They can be characterized in any way that is meaningful.* A few examples follow.

Body	Material Possessions	Money
Mind	Personal Growth and Healing	Golf
Spirit	Professional Development	Sex and Intimacy
	Financial Security	Status

Learning New Things	*Helen's List:*
Making a Difference	Creativity
Being Outdoors	Personal Health and Well Being
Loving Others	Marriage, Children and Family
Self-Expression	Home and Environment
	Spirituality and the Planet

Benjamin Franklin's 13 Virtues:

Temperance	Humility	Sincerity	Cleanliness	Resolution
Silence	Frugality	Justice	Tranquility	
Order	Industry	Moderation	Chastity	

The Franklin Planner's Suggestions for "Governing Values":

Family	Cultural/Educational
Company: Career	Spiritual/Humanitarian

After creating the list, the items can be ranked in order of relative importance; that is, *really* important ("A"), pretty important ("B"), not so important, but nice to have if I can get around to it ("C"). Use the table below to write down *and* rank your priorities.

Priorities
( )
( )
( )
( )
( )

Long-Range Goals

With this step complete, *set aside* this paperwork and start fresh with goal-setting. That's right. *Disregard* the list you have just made. Don't force its influence upon your goal-setting. Goal-setting works best, I believe, as a *parallel* process, when you do not set goals *based* on your priorities. Instead, you simply write down some goals, any goals you might feel passionate about, and *then* use your list of priorities later to check on how the goals fit them.

Let me explain with an example. It might be that physical health is "number one" in importance to you, but this should not dictate that you must set a major goal related to supporting your physical health. On the contrary, you may feel no need at all to change your established exercise routine. You may in fact wish to work in the coming year exclusively on career goals.

The point here is *awareness*. If you have chosen goals that fit into certain priority areas, can you live with that? Or should you go back to the drawing board and modify your goals based on what you know about your priorities?

Use the following table to jot down any goals which come to mind to which you feel drawn, or for which you have a passion. After you have completed 3-5 good long-range (five-year) goals, read them over and decide which priorities, if any, they might contribute to. Write them in the second column. Then take some time to reflect upon your list and decide if you can live with the choices you are making. If you can't, start over. If you can, proceed with breaking the goals into do-able chunks.

Goals	Relevant Priorities

Take each long-term goal and set short-term goals that will contribute to its completion. Then break each short-term goal down into do-able chunks.

You will need to make and complete several copies of the form below in order to address each goal fully. The final step will be to enter daily tasks in a calendar or daily planner.

Long Range Goal		Relevant Priorities	
Short-Term Goal			
A, B, C (Prioritize)	**Daily Tasks**		**Completion Dates**

As you choose your goals, remember the power that they hold. When you dare to articulate goals, your heart, mind, *and* your awareness opens to possibilities which might otherwise have eluded you. Then you can recognize opportunities that cross your path, and you are likely to take advantage of some of them. I recall listening to someone lecture about "visionary thinking" several years ago. She spoke about her desire to own a little red sports car. At first, she hesitated to even think about it, because she thought that the possibility of finding and affording one would be so remote. She finally gave herself permission to envision herself in that little red sports car, to see the image in all its detail. Within three weeks, she was driving it. The image had been so clear in her mind that when she glimpsed that car out of the corner of her eye in a dealer's lot, while driving down the highway, it virtually jumped out at her.

This stage of envisioning goals can be rich and exciting. Sadly, self sabotage**** can also rear its naughty head at this early stage. So be aware of the goals you set for yourself, make sure that they are your *own* goals and not things you have been told you "should" do or be, and make sure that you let yourself dream.

Now let's walk through an example. First, let's suppose a fictional fellow named Jerry came up with a list of priorities from the above example, as follows:

Priorities
( ) Body
( ) Mind
( ) Spirit

**** I will discuss self sabotage further in Step 5.

He then goes back and decides, which is most important to me of these three? And he prioritizes them using the letter system suggested.

Priorities
[B] Body
[C] Mind
[A] Spirit

Next, Jerry *sets aside* his priorities and sets four goals that come to mind about which he feels some passion. He will compare these with his priorities later.

Goals	Relevant Priorities
Put in a garden.	
Lose 25 pounds.	
Improve relations with my wife.	
Learn how to do spreadsheets.	

Then, he examines his goals and decides under which priorities they fit.

Goals	Relevant Priorities
1. Put in a garden.	Spirit (A) and Body (B)
2. Lose 25 pounds.	Body (B)
3. Improve relations with my wife.	Spirit (A) and Body (B)
4. Learn how to do spreadsheets.	Mind (C)

Jerry can see that he has chosen goals which fit well with his priorities. He is surprised to find that he has two goals that address his spiritual life, and is pleased about that. Based on his observations, he decides to keep and to work with these goals. Now he must expand upon each on in detail. One page that Jerry writes about his third goal appears on the following page.

Jerry will need to complete several of these sheets, in most cases more than one for *each* long range goal he sets. Then he can enter each item into his personal planner or calendar. It may take a number of short-term goals and many, many smaller tasks to complete a single long range goal. Breaking the process down increases your appreciation of exactly what is required to achieve something. Sometimes it causes us to re-think our goals before moving ahead with them.

Long Range Goal #3 *Improve relations with my wife.*	Relevant Priorities *Spirit and Body.*

| **Short Term Goal** *Make the commitment to have a "date" once a week.* ||

A,B,C (Priorities)	**Daily Tasks**	**Completion Dates**
A	*Agree upon a day of the week that works for both of us.*	*Tonight! 4/18, 10 p.m.*
A	*Start out doing things that <u>she</u> likes to do. Plan what we'll do one month ahead. Write it in the calendar!*	*4/19*
A	*Call to arrange for a babysitter.*	*4/19*
A	*Talk!*	*ongoing*

Time Management"

One of the most important lessons about time that I ever learned was the difference between "urgent" and "important," an idea advanced by Stephen Covey (1989). An urgent task is one which calls out for an immediate response: the phone rings, someone knocks on the door, you sever a limb in a horrible accident. Whether or not the event is important to you personally, it demands a response. Important tasks, on the other hand, may or may not be urgent, but they are tasks for which you have assigned a high value. Most people know these most important tasks in their hearts, especially when they quiet themselves. But if the important things ever knock loudly at your door, they only do so when they have been ignored repeatedly; and even then some people won't let themselves be distracted by them. It is up to you to make the time to attend to them, and in our day and age, with so much going on around us, this requires a deliberate effort.

Covey eloquently describes the relationship between important and urgent tasks in his "time management matrix" (1989, p. 151), which I have simplified on the following page. Any task, Covey explains, can be described in terms of its importance and its urgency. Those which are the most critical to attend to in order to achieve new goals for yourself are important and not urgent (cell #2). You can make them more urgent by incorporating time-limited tasks to support them in your daily routine. The outcomes of taking this deliberate step are well worth the effort.

Covey's Time Management Matrix	
I. IMPORTANT URGENT	**II.** **IMPORTANT** **NOT URGENT**
III. NOT IMPORTANT URGENT	**IV.** NOT IMPORTANT NOT URGENT

This has been a somewhat abbreviated look at goals and planning, but there is already a multitude of resources available. I personally am fond of the value-based Franklin Covey Day Planner system, but other viable options exist. Find one that fits *you.*

There are many other things to be said about time management. But the final message I feel compelled to leave you with is this: The most important thing you can do to keep yourself on the right track is to unceasingly *follow your Bliss.* This means remaining cognizant of and true to your goals, of course. But more importantly, it means maintaining an acute awareness of the Bliss that calls you each and every day in little ways. It is never too soon to begin listening to your heart when you feel pulled in a particular direction. Don't wait until you have fully figured out some major, over-reaching goal you might have fantasized about. If it exists, the little moments of Bliss along the way can be enormously helpful in guiding you there. Go ahead and call that person who has been on your mind. Sign up for that class you saw in the paper that piqued your interest. Apply for that job you saw advertised that made you tingle. Too many people rationalize their ways out of listening to their hearts, and who knows how great the losses may be. You have heard the arguments: I'm too busy, I'm not good enough, maybe later. Do it now.

Finally, be prepared to be surprised by your Bliss. Seemingly unrelated things may beckon you at the same time; let your imagination take hold. I am reminded of a seminar I facilitated and a woman who had a new paralegal degree and a love for birds. She was stumped. But she dared to share her passions with her peers and found that her combination of interests inspired their imaginations. Almost immediately, someone piped up: What about doing paralegal work for an organization like the Audubon Society? She loved the idea. It can be a challenge to trust the wisdom in Bliss, especially if you have never taken such a risk before, but the rewards can be immeasurable.

Where the Jobs Are

Classified ads comprise a portion of job leads, but a much smaller portion than most people realize -- and I believe it's growing smaller.   Most jobs come from "unadvertised" openings. It is important to approach the search for leads imaginatively.   I have included a worksheet to get you started. It begins on the following page, and I will elaborate on each part of it here.

But before reading any further, be sure to remember to think of *yourself* as your most valuable resource. Have you made a commitment to devote your time and talent to your search? And what about your family? Are they supportive of your career goals? Talk with them about what the job search will mean to the family in terms of time and tasks, and discuss what you will need from each other.

To Love You Is To *Know* You

Begin by making a list of everyone you know. This may be an overstatement; but don't underutilize this area! The people who know you best will be your best advocates and go that extra mile to inform you and promote you to people *they* know. The categories in the exercise are intended to stimulate your imagination and memory.

EXERCISE 8: **WHERE THE JOBS ARE**

Fill in the blanks with as many contacts and ideas as you can imagine. Track your progress in following up on these contacts.

Contacts	Dates Contacted
Friends (including school/college friends, neighbors, children's friends)	
Relatives	

Community Contacts (merchants, hairdresser, mail carrier, bank teller)	
Leisure Time Acquaintances (church, volunteer work, clubs, music/sports groups)	
Job Contacts (current and former co-workers, supervisors, customers, clients)	
Newspapers, Newsletters and Professional Journals	

Directories	
Radio and Television Listings	
Favorite Web Sites and E-mail Addresses	
Pet Organizations	

School Placement Offices/Resources	
State Agency Offices	
Private Agencies	
Networking and Support Groups	
Other	

Newspapers and Professional Journals
     Use newspapers creatively. Do not limit yourself to one newspaper. Get the major ones, but remember local ones and special interest papers and newsletters. Read the business section to keep abreast of what companies are opening up, expanding, doing well. Note names of people who might make good contacts. Sometimes you will find notices of people being appointed to positions in charge of hiring. Also read trade magazines and professional journals. If you don't subscribe, check them out at your public library.

Classified Ads
     Let me take a moment to say a few words about advertised openings. Be advised that it is a rare employer who will know exactly which applicant will best perform the work that needs to be done. It is *your* job to help the employer understand why you might be the best person for the position.
     Ads consist of two main parts: job *requirements* (what the job requires you to do) and *qualifications* (what the employer *thinks* he or she needs from a job candidate to get the job done). Before even considering the qualifications requested, study the job requirements and ask yourself, *can* I do this job? Is there any way that I can do this job well? If the answer is no, then don't bother pursuing it. But if you can honestly answer yes, and if you would *like* to give the job a try, or at least find out more about it, *then* study the list of preferred qualifications. If your particular blend of talents and credentials are not a perfect match with the employer's best guess as to what the job requires, then make it your task to persuade the employer, just as you yourself are convinced, how your

talents and know-how equip you to excel at the position. Use Exercise 9, below, to get a handle on responding to classified ads.

EXERCISE 9: **RESPONDING TO CLASSIFIED ADS**

Paste the classified ad that interests you in the left hand column. Read the ad, and pull out any items which pertain to job requirements. List them under the Job Requirements column. Address each item with how you may be uniquely equipped to perform the function, writing your ideas in the next column, under "Can I do this job?" Once you have satisfied yourself that you can do this job, read the ad again for desired qualifications. List these in the second column under "Qualifications." Finally, note how you can meet the qualifications.

Classified Ad	Job Requirements	Can I do this job?
[Paste classified ad here.]	1. 2. 3. 4.	1. 2. 3. 4.
	Qualifications	How do I measure up? Can I compensate for weaknesses?
	1. 2. 3. 4.	1. 2. 3. 4.

Note the example below.

Classified Ad	Job Requirements	Can I do this job?
WANTED: EMPLOYMENT SPECIALIST Coordinate summer jobs program for inner city youth. Develop network of companies hiring. Coordinate advisory board. Teach job seeking skills. Supervise interns. B.A. in vocational rehab. and 1-3 yrs supervisory exp. M.A. preferred. Must have own transportation. Call...	1. *Skills in program coordination (well organized, good communicator,)* 2. *Ability to work with employers/ sales skills.* 3. *Knowledge of job-seeking skills. Teaching ability.* 4. *Supervisory skills.*	1. *Yes! I'm well organized. I speak & write well. Held offices in clubs.* 2. *Yes! Eager for this opportunity. Top cookie sales for Girl Scouts. Maturity & poise.* 3. *Yes! Completed class @ college, incl. internship at Rehab. Office.* 4. *Yes! Leader, pull my weight, good communicator, can inspire & motivate others. Experienced!*
	Qualifications	**How do I measure up? Can I compensate for weaknesses?**
	1. *B.A. (M.A. preferred) in Voc. Rehabilitation* 2. *Car.* 3. *1-3 yrs supervisory exp.*	1. *B.A. in anthropology. Related classes. Good rapport w/kids. Quick study. Enthusiastic!* 2. *Easy!* 3. *Supervised & trained up to 8 wait persons in restaurant, 2 yrs.*

As in any sales task, you will need to anticipate objections and prepare responses. Practice, and take your "pitch" to the employer. I will discuss contacting and interviewing employers further in the upcoming two sections.

Directories

Directories are another useful source. Telephone companies publish not only the familiar Yellow Pages, but also a Business-to-Business directory and a Human Services Yellow Pages. Have your librarian point our directories specific to your industry and your geographical area as well. You can also tap into "Pro-Phone," a nationwide computerized telephone book available at many libraries.

Radio and Television

Radio and television stations, including cable stations, occasionally run listings as well as special informational programs for job seekers. (Often these appear during the wee hours of the morning.)

The World Wide Web

The fastest growing job hunting networks can be accessed through the World Wide Web on the Internet. If you are not on-line at work or at home, your librarian or your local state job service may be able to acquaint you with the process of accessing information and sending and receiving electronic mail. Web sites are growing and changing every day and are far too numerous to list here. Find your favorites and list them.

Pet Organizations

Many organizations may be able to help. Chambers of Commerce keep data on businesses and organizations, and sometimes they sponsor get-togethers that offer networking opportunities.

Contact the professional associations and nonprofit organizations with which you might have a connection. Many social service organizations offer job search assistance of various kinds. Look for private industry councils, regional employment boards, state funded career centers, and also groups like the YMCA and religious organizations.

School Placement Offices/Resources

College, university and high school placement offices usually offer free services and leads to their alumni, as well as networking opportunities. Make an appointment to look through the resources.

State Agency Offices

State employment agencies and each state's vocational rehabilitation agency are specifically designed to offer resources to support your job search. They offer classes, career counseling, job listings, and may be able to put your resumé on the Internet.

Private Agencies

Private employment agencies are listed in the yellow pages and classified ads. You will find temporary placement agencies, which give you opportunities to "test-drive" companies while bringing home some income. Head-hunting agencies are usually specific to particular industries; make sure you know the fees.

Networking Groups

Networking and support groups have sprouted up all over the place. Some require a small fee to help cover expenses. Check your phone book, churches, local employment agencies, Rotary clubs or the chamber of commerce for listings.

What else?

In addition to making and using contact lists, be sure you also look around you. Bulletin Boards are everywhere. Look for postings in churches, schools, laundromats, grocery stores, libraries, offices, and so on. Many companies post internally before advertising to the general public. Have others keep ears and eyes open for you. Also look for signs and new construction in areas where you would like to work.

Finally, get leads from your leads. Every time you make a contact, you are just a question away from another contact. Most people are happy to share ideas with you, especially if your enthusiasm is genuine. (Don't *you* love it when you make somebody's day just by sharing some information?)

You may be able to add more to the list. Grab extra paper and write your ideas down.

As you research and acquire leads, decide how to best pursue them. Begin with what you can do *today* to support your change to a more meaningful career. Write the daily tasks that you set for yourself into your calendar/planner, and then *act*.

Follow up frequently. Results will come from narrowing your field and from persistently focusing on and putting more energy into fewer, better leads, and developing relationships with people as you pursue those leads. You will find the approach much more fruitful than tossing your resumé around like confetti and hoping for someone to notice it and court you. Remember, quality over quantity is the name of the game.

Using the Telephone

A woman stares out her kitchen window, periodically glancing first at the clock ticking dangerously close to five p.m. and then back at the telephone perched on the counter. It seems to taunt her. Finally, she ushers her tense body to sit before the cold, impersonal phone. Time passes. She refuses to let herself answer to those pleas to turn on Oprah, fold the laundry, get supper started. No, she will make this call if it kills her. And suddenly, she surrenders and watches in panic as her fingers obey her and begin to dial. "Please don't answer. Please don't answer," a little voice silently begs.

"Management Associates."

[Deep breath.] "I'd like to speak with Personnel, please."

"May I ask what this is regarding?"

"Uh, yes. I saw your ad in the paper -- you have a job?"

"I'm sorry, ma'am. We're only accepting resumés at this time. No calls."

The phone is back in its cradle, and her face falls into her hands. She has done it. She can tell her friends, her counselor, herself. She tried, and she doesn't have to carry the guilt anymore. But she is still preoccupied with a deep sense of failure.

This is not a lesson on how to do or not do a cold call. It is an appeal to common sense which screams out: Why should anyone subject herself to this kind of torture?

Just as I urge people to follow Bliss, I also encourage them to stay within a reasonable level of comfort. Call when you feel excited about calling. Remember our fictional story about Jane, who dug herself into a hole trying to become more assertive, only to find that the assertiveness *grew* from her immersion in the things that she loved? After making the list of "everyone you know," which we discussed in the previous section, begin making contacts, but begin where you feel most at home and most comfortable. Introductions will naturally branch out from there, and you will be much more effective in your contacts and less likely to procrastinate when you feel self assured and confident.

That said, it is certainly true that the telephone is a direct and efficient way to contact a company. But many of us are intimidated by the phone and underutilize it. A prevalent fear seems to be, "Won't I seem pushy?" Remember: It is not *whether* you call that makes you pushy, it is *how you handle* the call. If you are a sensitive and courteous caller, people will appreciate your show of interest and in many cases will be more than happy to answer your questions.

I emphasize five rules for effective telephone use:

(1)   Be prepared.
(2)   Be somebody.
(3)   Be painfully courteous.
(4)   Don't hang up hand up empty-handed;
       try to get some kind of commitment.
(5)   Follow up.

1. Be Prepared

Know why you are calling and what you want to **say** *before* you pick up the phone. Make a brief, confident presentation   that   does   not   unnecessarily

EXAMPLE 14: SAMPLE TELEPHONE SCRIPT

Good morning. This is _____ calling for _____. Is (Mr./Ms.) _____ available?

Hello, (Mr./Ms.)_____. My name is _____. I'm a _____ (e.g., position title), and I've learned from _____ that you are currently looking to add some people to your field offices in _____ and _____. Do you have two or three minutes?

[If "No"] Fine. When would be a good time to call back?

[If "Yes"] Great! I was excited to hear about your expansion. I am familiar with your work, and I have been impressed with your track record. Could you tell me if you have prepared a schedule for conducting interviews? I would love to come in and talk with you about your needs and what I have to offer. When would be the best time for you? [You may need to respond to questions here about your qualifications. Don't waste the person's time if s/he does not ask -- you can cover it during the interview.]

Where are you located?

Thank you for your time. I really look forward to seeing you next Thursday. What materials would you like me to bring?

Okay, I will see you on Thursday at three p.m. at your office. Thanks again!

burden the recipient of the call. If you feel a need to call, but have no idea what to say, don't bother calling until you have figured it out. Otherwise, you will waste others' time as well as your own. (This may be a useful rule of thumb in your personal life as well!)

You may find a script helpful, so I have included a sample on the previous page. If you don't like using a script, then at least jot down the questions you wish to ask and the things you want to be sure to say, and keep pen and paper handy to take down the information. Don't count on your memory! (What if someone gives you a lengthy address or spells out a fifteen-letter, foreign name?) You will also need to be prepared to answer questions about yourself. Have a resumé at your fingertips and perhaps some notes about how you might answer key questions.

2. Be Somebody

Don't say, "I am calling to find out about job openings." Instead, try something like, "Hi, this is Joe Somebody calling for Mary Employer. Is Ms. Employer available?" Or perhaps, "This is Joe Somebody calling. Larry Coverletter suggested I give the clinical director a call. Could you give me the correct spelling of the director's name? Ida Boss? Thank you. Is Ms. Boss in?" You will run a much lower risk of being "screened out" and you will sound much more confident and in control.

3. Be Painfully Courteous

Show your appreciation for every piece of information (as you write it all down) and for the help you receive, from the receptionist on up. (The receptionist *may* be the most powerful individual in the firm! Know her name, too.) Being courteous, by the way, does not mean immediately agreeing to hang up so that you can wait for hours for a return phone call. You can be courteous, kind and assertive at the same time. Try an approach like this: "I know that Ms. Boss is very busy, but I may be difficult to reach and I don't want her to waste a call. Can you give me some times when I might try to call her back?" Then, make sure you follow up when you say you will.

4. Get *some* kind of commitment.

That commitment may be as small as getting the person to agree to your sending a resumé in the mail. Who is going to refuse that? There is a continuum of things you can get out of a phone call. Try for high on the list first, if you dare. (You will have to trust your gut.) Then, work your way down. Ask for:

- a job offer (a rare occurrence, but you never know);
- a job interview;
- an opportunity to check back later and inquire about openings;
- another job lead or contact; and/or
- an opportunity to send a resumé or other material.

5. Follow up.

If the employer suggests that you call back in three weeks or six months, write a note to yourself immediately and follow through as promised. Send materials you have promised right away, then follow up with a phone call. Thank-you notes will always give you an edge, even if it is only to thank someone for taking a few minutes to speak with you.

Interviewing

Most interview questions serve not only to collect information on skills and qualifications, but also to reveal the applicant's motives, values, and working style. Many applicants, however, only respond to questions literally, providing facts but perhaps missing opportunities to respond fully to the employer's need to get to know the person behind the information. I do not need to tell you the facts about yourself and your qualifications; however, I can help to de-mystify some commonly asked interview questions by exploring what employers *really* want to know when they pose them.

"Have you ever done this kind of work before?" The interviewer really wants to know how quickly you will be up and running in the job. "Yes" would be a literal response, but it's not enough. Tell when and where you have done the work, briefly, and add what you enjoyed about it, or highlight an achievement. If the answer is "No," don't stop there, either. Share some experience that was similar in some way, or at the very least your ability to learn quickly.

"Why do you want to work here?" In other words, what is your motive, and what can you tell me that I would enjoy hearing about how wonderful *we* are? The employer may be asking either or both. Convey your enthusiasm for the position, honestly and with your own style. Don't answer why you want *a* job, but why you want *this* job. (For example, you want to expand your skills, you are attracted to the company's reputation for excellent training, and you're wild about widgets.)

"Why did you leave your last job?" Here the interviewer wants reassurance. Are you going to repeat an unwanted action -- quit, or perform poorly so the employer will have to fire you? Whatever happened and however horrible, reassure the employer *through your self assured manner* that you won't be a trouble-maker. Answer honestly, and be brief. Don't go into a long-winded description or debate -- by trying to convince the interviewer that you were right and your former boss was wrong. This burdens the employer with unnecessary details and makes her feel that you are less in control. It also uses up valuable time better spent talking about your assets.

"What are your salary requirements?" Of course the interviewer wants to know if he can afford you, but he may be asking this question for a couple of other reasons. Perhaps it is a new position, and he lacks information about the usual salaries for this line of work. Or perhaps he wants to know how low you will go as you begin to negotiate. Put the ball back into the interviewer's court momentarily by asking for the salary *range*, and *then* choose what you feel is a reasonable figure. You might even choose a little high, but show that you are open to negotiate. If he won't give you a range, then you name a range, and negotiate from there. You may want to factor in the potential for advancement or the annual review process. Whatever you do, know what your absolute minimum needs are before you even go into the interview, and don't settle for less.

"What are your greatest strengths?" Here the employer will learn not only what you can do, but also how you feel about yourself and how confidently and honestly you can present yourself. Again, share what is most relevant to the job in question. This does not come naturally to most of us, but practice makes perfect. Practice with your friends a few times before the interview.

"What are your greatest weaknesses?" The employer is really asking the same thing here, but from the other side. After all, our greatest strengths are also our greatest weaknesses, just viewed from another angle. Understand that weaknesses provide clues to dominant qualities, which serve you in a positive ways. Be honest, and don't apologize. Show how you accommodate for "weakness." For example, "I sometimes get so absorbed in my work that I lose touch with people around me. This means I get a lot done [strength], but I do need to make a point of checking in with the people on my team to make sure to maintain good working relationships [accommodation]." --Instead of, "My co-workers are always telling me that I am rude and detached."

"Do you have any health problems?" You are required by law to answer *only as it pertains to the job requirements.* There is no need to share information that is not relevant. If you have seizures that are controlled with medication, for example, share this information only if your personality demands it. That is, share it only if you will be so tied up on knots for "hiding it" that you won't be able to perform well and may even exacerbate your condition. What the employer really wants to know is if you are dependable, or if she should expect a lot of absences. Do tell if you have a medical condition that restricts you from performing the job, then suggest an accommodation, or a few options, if possible. (For example, if flashing lights give you migraine headaches, can your phone be altered?) If you have a disability or health concern that you feel could generate some issues one way or another on the job, read up on the Americans with Disabilities Act (ADA).^{******}

"Tell me about yourself." Here is an instance where the employer seems to be asking for personal data. In fact, embarking on a personal story unrelated to the job at hand is *not* the way to respond to this one. Share special interests or hobbies *as they pertain to your suitability* to the position, company, and/or milieu in question. Tell, for example, how you have established quick rapport with people through your ham radio hobby, or how you have used your creative talents in designing your own clothes. Let your personality *shine through* your discussion of job related material.

"Do you have any questions for me?" Here, the employer is courteously letting you ask about something he might have omitted, but chances are he is asking this question at the end of an interview. Be brief, but memorable. Share something important that will help the interviewer remember the kind of person you are. Some

---

******This material extends beyond the scope of this book; however, Rich Pimentel and Michael J. Lotito, Esq. have prepared what I believe are the best, most readable materials available on this topic. See the reference list for more information.

questions that can elicit valuable information for you include the following:

- What do you think is required for someone to excel in this position?
- How did the position come to be open?
- With whom would I be working?
- How did *you* come to work here? What do you like about working here?
- May I see where I would be working?

STEP FIVE:
MUSTERING THE COURAGE TO FOLLOW BLISS

Your work is yours to choose
and the choice is as wide as your mind.
Nothing more is possible.
Nothing less is human.
-- Ayn Rand

I've felt compelled to follow my Bliss for much of my life, but it has not been easy. I recall moments when my greatest enemy has been myself, when I have chickened out instead of moving forward. No matter how clearly I knew what needed to be done, that nasty little voice of self sabotage taunted me. "You're dreaming! Get real! You haven't got a chance!" And I listened. Each of us knows that voice which admonishes, "You shouldn't. You don't deserve it," or the one which insists, "You can't. You're not good enough."

You should. You can. You *must.*

Let me share the story of someone with enormous strength of spirit who was able to find great success in life and work in spite of the fact that hardly anyone believed in him -- and, some might argue, justifiably so.

A young man I'll call Fred walked into a "last stop" career placement office one day after meeting with what felt to him like one rejection after another. My colleague described him as a young man who had an infectious smile, a clear sense of purpose, and some cognitive limitations. (He bore the label of mental retardation.) He had been to several public agencies requesting assistance, each time insisting that he wanted to be a doctor. Repeatedly, he met with varying degrees of incredulity and disparagement, and in the end, encouragement to get a fast food or housekeeping job. To his credit, he kept going until he found Bernie.

Bernie and I worked in the same program and were accustomed to stories such as his. We had been surprised enough times by people to learn never to second-guess them. Our approach was to meet the person where he was, trust the wisdom in the person's dreams, and support him however we could. Without attempting to discourage him, Bernie openly discussed with Fred the educational challenges that he faced. He explained that doctors required many years of education and suggested beginning by breaking the goal down into do-able chunks. The first step was to complete a high school diploma. Fred was excited. He signed up for a G.E.D. program. Bernie also found that Fred didn't know a lot about the health care industry, and together he and Fred explored ways to learn more about it. Fred decided to volunteer at a local hospital.

Through his volunteer work, Fred learned of a job opening for an orderly at the hospital. He applied for the job, and because of the good reputation he had built during his time volunteering, the staff were thrilled to hire him.

The next time Bernie saw Fred, he showed up at the career office dressed in a white orderly suit, glowing, as he proudly announced, "I'm a doctor!"

Fred believed in his dream, and with persistence he realized it. In this case, one might say that he had been naming it prematurely, but this is the way of Bliss. It can work in mysterious ways for all of us. It may not be clear for a long time where our heart is leading us, but if we simply trust the process, it will not fail us. There may be a job just over the horizon that *you* cannot name, because it is just as much a mystery to you as being an orderly was to Fred. Fred followed the nearest star, and it led him right where he belonged.

Trust the process. I've heard the phrase many times, but it is a useful reminder. Give yourself time and room to stumble. Surround yourself with people who believe in you and can support you in your process.

Remember, too, that change is always painful no matter how "right," because it is always accompanied by loss. This brings up the paradox which exists in following Bliss. It is tempting to assume that the task of following Bliss is an indulgent and pleasing one, requiring little effort. In fact, it can be a most agonizing endeavor.

I recall as a young person listening to a sermon in a small-town Catholic church. The priest was a guest speaker -- a young, handsome fellow invited to inspire the young men of the parish into the priesthood. I am sure the elders of the congregation viewed his language and approach as somewhat unseemly, but his message reached me in a powerful way. He told the story of his "calling," characterizing himself as a typical young person whose first reaction to the blessed event was a vehement, "Oh, shit!" And it was not a groundless, gut reaction. He knew that he would face many sacrifices and demands, but he also knew that he could not fulfill his purpose in any other way.

The moments of ecstasy which accompany the fulfillment of a clear sense of purpose are balanced with moments of agony. Both contribute to richness in life and ensure our active participation here on earth.

On the other hand, work is not meant to equal drudgery. Work is what we do, and choosing work that feeds our soul is no luxury -- *it is a responsibility.* If you have a gift lying dormant because you feel that using it would somehow be "cheating," think again. You may be committing a great injustice not only to yourself, but also to your community and the world.

Beware Self Sabotage

Suppose you know all of this. You "get it." You know what needs to be done. But you still can't seem to do the right thing. You are sabotaging your own success.

Of all the demographic segments of the population we might point to as having the least promise of ever finding and keeping meaningful and satisfying employment, one stands head and shoulders above the rest: the *discouraged* worker. Discouraged people find ways to sabotage their success every step of the way. And the one thing that I believe discouraged people lack most, once again, is imagination. The surest way to get out of a rut is to *see things differently* and to *see different things.* As we have heard many times, we need to learn to see another side, a silver lining, the rest of the picture. This simply requires imagination, and any exercise that stretches imagination can help here. Try the one on the following page.

Often it takes an enormous amount of imagination to follow Bliss, but it insists upon our attention. What is it telling you, or asking of you? Take your questions to a lump of clay, or write a fairy tale. Imagination thrives in places such as these, and a peer or expressive therapist can be an invaluable aid in discovering and learning from the rich images which live there.

Sometimes self sabotage results from deep-seated feelings of being undeserving, or put another way, an

---

EXERCISE 10: **STRETCHING IMAGINATION**

Make two marks on the floor: "Point A" and "Point B." Then try to imagine different ways to move between the two. Walk, run, skip, hop, cartwheel, slither, sneak, somersault, tango, ice skate, bungee-jump, impersonate a crab -- each attempt stretches your imagination further. Get others to join you in this game. They will inspire your imagination tremendously, help you to *see things differently* and to see things you had not before imagined. Then use the *same faculty* -- imagination -- to work out an obstacle to your career path. Perhaps at first glance your resistance to picking up that phone *looks like* mere laziness. Can you imagine what else might be entering this equation? It may *seem* that a prospective employer "just doesn't like me." What else may be part of this picture?

---

inability to *imagine* ourselves as deserving souls. We may know on an intellectual level that "everyone" deserves happiness and fulfillment, but on an emotional level this can be excruciatingly difficult to imagine or accept. I appeal to people's sense of responsibility in these cases. Don't do it because you want to or because it "feels good"; do it because *it is your work.* It is your responsibility. You are called. Don't *short*-change the world. *Change* the world! "Nothing less is human."

Some people simply cannot tolerate *change.* The first step to overcoming this obstacle is to recognize it for what it is. Once you understand the nature of a problem and admit to it, you can put it outside of yourself and work with it. Find ways to *ease* yourself into change and to become more comfortable with it. Take risks in small steps. Remember, too, that routine is a good thing. Don't just cast routine into the wind; build *new* routines to replace the old. Eventually they will become familiar and comforting as well.

Another example of self sabotage sounds like this: "I couldn't take that job. It's so wonderful. I'm sure someone *else* wants it/deserves it/could excel at it more than I." Would we really give our Bliss away? Some people would. But the sad truth is, these fantasies about other people are rarely, if ever, true. Everyone's Bliss is a little different. Not everyone wants to be president. Just ask a few people, in all seriousness. Most of us just want to tell the president what to do. Not everyone possesses a passion to be a rock 'n' roll star, either.

I remember working with a young woman, who had a developmental disability, to establish some career-life goals. Do you know what her deepest, most secret dream was? To have an apartment of her own. As an outsider, I could see that the goal might require some planning and work, but it was absolutely within her reach. We are all provided with the tools and strength we require to achieve our deepest desires. We have everything we need to succeed, and never are we called to a purpose beyond the reach of our abilities.

Finding an Image of Strength

There is a simple method I use to rise out of states of vulnerability and discouragement. I sit with the ill feelings and let an image emerge, then I work with the image so that I may better appreciate its complexity and how it serves me. By "working with the image," I am referring to drawing or sculpting it, or writing about it.

I remember one of the first times I used this exercise. I was teaching a class of first-year graduate students in the expressive therapies. It was about two months into the semester -- about the time when, as always happens with group dynamics, the "honeymoon was over." This can be a painful time of learning for anyone who facilitates groups regularly, and, as I was a relative novice on the faculty, it was painful for me. In short, I had not met the expectations of some of the students. As a core teacher of expressive therapies, I was an art and music therapist but not a skilled psychodramatist, and I could not compensate for the perceived inadequacy. The students realized that I was not their "perfect mother." In their minds, I had failed them.

At the time, I was preparing to teach an intensive weekend. I decided to try working with the image of weakness which loomed before me so large, and to see if that would lead me to a different image, one of strength, that I could arm myself with before the next class. I felt I needed defensive armor.

The image of weakness which came to me was that of a sponge. It fit my style of facing conflict to a tee. I regarded the sponge and thought, "Yes, this is me. I don't deflect like a shield, nor do I attack like a sword. I soak criticisms in with every fiber of my being. It is pure agony. The soaking process is not paralyzing, but it does require pause and takes a lot of time. I absorb every accusation, every glance, every word, every insult, fully and completely. I slow down." Staying with the image, I considered, "But I am never destroyed, and I never lose the integrity of my shape. A sponge is malleable, flexible. It can be manipulated, influenced -- but a sponge is not clay. The impressions cannot force me into something that I am not." And so, the very *same* image which I felt described my weakness became my image of strength as well. The exercise rejuvenated me, and I was able to conclude that intensive weekend class having gained a new level of respect from the students. It may seem a bit of a mystery how I gained that respect, since I did not earn in a day the credential they felt they required of me. I expect that the change had everything to do with the way I carried myself and presented myself, *just as I was.*

Images of self sabotage must be dealt with again and again in our lives, for they tend to recur. But the better acquainted we become with imagination, the easier the way through. Those one-sided fantasies we have like, "My boss hates me because I am bad" can be expanded into "I participate in a dance with this person, a complex person. I now know better what makes this person tick. I can let go of my defensive attitude now."

CLOSING REMARKS

In the preceding pages, I have tried to walk you, the reader, through a process of reflection, self-inventorying and career-life planning. Along the way I have challenged some popular career counseling methodologies and offered a perspective shaped by my approach to the practice of career counseling as an art and a spiritual quest.

My goal has been to update, simplify, and de-mystify the process of career-life planning and to challenge and inspire you. But more than anything else, I hope that I have managed to ignite your imagination and bolster your courage a bit. I hope also that I have conveyed my personal faith in all people and their diverse talents and my belief that when it comes to career niches there are no hopeless cases.

My final counsel to you is simple: When you become confused along your career path and wonder which direction to take, let yourself be guided by the wisdom which judges or measures the rightness of a thing -- a decision, a choice, or an act -- by the magnitude of passion or excitement which accompanies it.

Let your imagination be inspired, and muster the courage to follow your Bliss. They have not yet failed me, and I trust they will not fail you.

ABOUT THE AUTHOR

Helen Nienhaus Barba is an expressive therapist, a Registered Art Therapist (A.T.R.), and a nationally certified Clinical Mental Health Counselor (CCMHC) currently living in Prior Lake, Minnesota, where she is pursuing a doctorate and working hard at raising four young children with her husband, John. The contents of this book emerged in large part from material acquired through her private career counseling practice, CareerLife Visions. She operated the practice in Massachusetts between 1988 and 1996, and was able to guide many people through the process of following their Bliss. Ms. Barba co-authored the text *Minstrels of Soul: Intermodal Expressive Therapies* with Paolo Knill and Margo Fuchs in 1993.

REFERENCES

Barba, H. (1988). *A Psychology of Recurring Imagery* (Master's thesis). Cambridge: Lesley College Graduate School.

Barlow, E., Jr. (1995, September). *Creating the Future: The Journey Towards the Next Millennium.* Presentation at Mount Wachusett Community College, Gardner, Massachusetts.

Bissonnette, D. (1994). *Beyond Traditional Job Development: The Art of Creating Opportunity.* Northridge, California: Milt Wright Associates, Inc. (1-800-626-3939)

Bolles, R. (1994). *What Color Is Your Parachute?* San Francisco: Ten Speed Press.

Boyan, W. (1995, October). *Keeping America Competitive.* Paper published by the National Alliance of Businesses.

Campbell, J. (1988). *Joseph Campbell and the Power of Myth*, with Bill Moyers. Betsy Sue Flowers, ed. New York: Doubleday.

Covey, S. (1989). *The Seven Habits of Highly Efficient People.* New York: Simon and Schuster, Inc.

Gelfman, P., Ed. (1994). *Minnesota Job Seeker's Sourcebook* (2nd Ed.). Minnetonka, Minnesota: Resource Publishing Group, Inc. (612) 545-5980.

Hillman, J. (1977). *Re-Visioning Psychology.* New York: Harper and Row.

Jeffers, S. (1987). *Feel the Fear and Do It Anyway.* New York: Harcourt Brace Janovich.

Knill, P.; Barba, H.; & Fuchs, Margo (1993). *Minstrels of Soul: Intermodal Expressive Therapy.* Toronto: Palmerston Press.

Lowman, R. (1991). *The Clinical Practice of Career Assessment: Interests, Abilities and Personality.* Washington, D.C.: American Psychological Association, 1991.

McAuliffe, G. (1993, Winter). Career as an imaginative quest. *American Counselor,* 13-36.

McNiff, S. (1988). *Fundamentals of Art Therapy.* Springfield, IL: Charles C. Thomas.

Pimentel, R. and M. Lotito, Esq. (1992). *The Americans with Disabilities Act: Making the ADA Work for You.* (2nd Ed.) Chatsworth, CA: Milt Wright& Associates, 1992. This and other excellent materials are available by calling 1-800-629-3939.

Rand, A. (1957). *Atlas Shrugged.* New York: Random House.

Reich, R. (1988). *Tales of a New America.* Vintage Books.

McCarthy, B. (Producer & Director). (1991). *Sam Keen: Your Mythic Journey, with Bill Moyers* [videotape]. New York: Public Affairs Television, Inc. Color, 58 minutes.

Siegel, Bernie, M.D. (1986). *Love, Medicine and Miracles.* New York: Harper & Row.

Sher, Barbara (1994). *I Could Do Anything If Only I Knew What It Was.* New York: Delacorte Press.

_____. (1979). *WishCraft.* New York: Viking Press.

TimeQuest Self-Paced Time and Life Management System (1998). Franklin Covey Tools for Highly Effective Living. (To order, call 1-800-351-1492.)

Wegmann, R.; Chapman, R. & Johnson, M. (1989). *Work in the New Economy.* (Revised Ed.) Alexandria, VA: American Association for Counseling and Development and Indianapolis: JIST Works, Inc. (co-publishers).

INDEX

McNiff, 7, 9, 13, 75
myth, 29, 30
objective, 22, 77, 78, 80, 83, 84, 93, 97
planner, 95, 121, 125, 129, 141
planning, 3, 9, 36, 43, 60, 98, 112, 115, 117, 118, 129, 160, 163
rage, 45
Rand, 155
recommendation, 90, 104-106
references, 9, 83, 90, 95, 97, 98, 101, 103-105
resume, 18, 78, 93, 101, 104-106, 108
sabotage, 123, 155, 158, 160, 162
salary, 150
Sher, 49
Siegel, 23
strengths, 20, 36, 37, 39, 84, 86, 96, 105, 151
success, 11, 21, 23, 34, 77, 104, 113, 155, 158
talents, 9, 11, 20, 28, 50, 59-61, 66, 68, 78, 80, 81, 91, 94, 107, 112-114, 136, 137, 152, 163
telephone, 9, 105, 139, 143-145
time management, 127-129
unemployment, 24, 27, 102
values, 9, 11, 15, 29, 30, 49-51, 56-60, 80, 118, 119, 149
weaknesses, 37, 39, 137, 138, 151

Printed in the United States
942200001B

9 781581 127461